629.22 Engel, Lyle Kenyon
E
The complete
motorcycle book

the complete
MOTORCYCLE
book

produced by
Lyle Kenyon Engel

text by
Deke Houlgate

Four Winds Press New York

Photo Credits

American Motorcycle Association, pp. 115, 116, 117, 119, 120, 123.

Bill Krause Sportcycles, p. 80.

"On Any Sunday," Bruce Brown Productions, pp. 30, 70, 71, 113, 125, 128, 129, 130, 132, 143.

Escape Country Recreation Park, p. 164.

Honda, pp. 157, 158.

Suzuki, pp. 134, 146, 150.

Yamaha, pp. 20, 23, 28, 35, 36, 37, 38, 40, 43, 45, 46, 50, 51, 56, 58, 61, 66, 73, 78, 80, 82, 83, 84, 85, 87, 88, 92, 96, 155.

Library of Congress Cataloging in Publication Data
Engel, Lyle Kenyon.
  The complete motorcycle book.

  1. Motorcycles. 2. Motorcycling. 3. Motorcycle racing. I. Title.
TL440.E5   629.22'75   73–88085
ISBN 0–590–17268–9

Published by Four Winds Press
A Division of Scholastic Magazines, Inc. New York, N.Y.
Copyright © 1974 by Lyle Kenyon Engel
All rights reserved.
Printed in the United States of America
Library of Congress Catalog Card Number: 73–88085

2   3   4   5   78   77   76   75

Contents

Foreword

Motorcycling is a pleasure, a thrill. It gives a person a great feeling when he knows he is able to master the power of an incredible machine. But it is not only for these reasons that the motorcycle has become an important part of American life.

The sport of motorcycling has come of age in the United States because the human being in a free society has a strong drive to assert himself. He wants to say, "I did it myself."

Riding a motorcycle is like flying an airplane. Motorcycles and airplanes are two of man's most demanding inventions. Learning to operate them gives a person the ultimate feeling of knowledge —to be able to control or master an awesome power. Becoming skillful later is all just a part of it. The baby delights in learning to walk, but he is even happier when he starts to run.

I have participated in many sports, but none of them gave me the personal satisfaction that motorcycling gives me. To make all of the swift, precise movements together that you must when operating a motorcycle, I believe, gives the rider unconsciously the feeling he is more capable than other persons who can't or won't ride a motorcycle.

That is why the phrase "When motorcycling gets in your blood, you can't get it out" is true. Those of us who know it are proud of it.

This book by my friend, Deke Houlgate, I hope, will encourage others who have never tried motorcycling to realize someday a little more of their own capabilities. May the greatest sport on wheels make their lives a little more complete!

Happy Landings,
Evel Knievel

World champion Roger De-Coster of Belgium shows good jumping form during a European moto-cross race.

A Swedish rider, left, two Russians (#15 and #16) and a West German muscle their way through an uphill curve at the Austrian world moto-cross championship event.

1
Taking It From the Top

Motorcycles and automobiles came into being for the same basic reason. Man, the tinkerer, wanted to perfect a self-propelled vehicle. Early automobile inventors started with wagon technology, which was fairly advanced, having undergone centuries of updating. The motorbike was based upon the more exciting, adventurous vehicle known as the velocipede, or bicycle.

It seems amazing that only one hundred years ago a far-seeing engineer was ridiculed or punished for talking loosely about the practical use of a self-propelled vehicle, but it did happen. There were a few inventive geniuses who built self-propelled wagons, bicycles and tricycles, but the products they made were largely experimental. Unfortunately for us, there was little written about those early attempts to make self-propelled cars and bikes, and only a few of the crude experiments survive today in museums and private collections.

It wasn't until the 1890s that the horseless carriage became sufficiently known by the public at large for a magazine to be published called *The Horseless Age*. The uncertain direction of the motor vehicle industry was revealed in the first issue of that periodical in 1895 as automobiles (four wheels) and motorcycles (two or three wheels) were poorly identified anywhere inside the covers. The self-propelled vehicles of the new generation were called variously *kerosene carriage, electric wagon, motor road wagon, petroleum carriage, vapor-driven horseless carriage, motor trap, business wagon, steam carriage* or *ether bicycle.*

There were six three-wheel machines and five four-wheelers depicted in the issue that were called *motocycles.* The word *automobile* did not come into general use until 1899.

Early "motorcycles" were mostly powered by steam, because the use of steam engines was more than one hundred years old at the time, but some of the early vehicles burned kerosene, and some were propelled through generation of hot air or electricity. One was set in motion by means of a coiled spring. All these self-propelled carts were crude compared to today's machines, but the great number of them and their variety of design left no doubt that the transportation revolution that was eventually to find man walking on the moon in the twentieth century was under way.

It would take a very wise student of history to decide which came first, the motorcycle or the automobile, partly because they were both developed at about the same time. The real reason we know so little about early automobile history and less about motorcycles of the same era is that the world at large paid little attention to either. We can only guess that three-wheeled motorcycles powered by steam were in somewhat general use in the 1830s in England. We think we know this because a drawing made in 1831 has been preserved that shows a park scene in which a number of steam-powered tricycles are puffing about. One expert on the subject speculates that artists of that day knew too little about engineering concepts to "invent" the steamcycle for their pictures, and that they must have had real models to copy.

Another historian guesses there were about one hundred steamcycles in use by 1830 in England because both steam power and bicycle technology were well developed at that time.

Inventing a motorcycle in those very early days was a difficult task. First someone had to invent an engine that would work reliably. Then someone else had to come up with the idea that it could be used to propel a bicycle or a wagon. Still other inventive processes remained—for instance, how to modify the engine so it didn't have to be anchored to the ground near a tank of fuel or a reservoir of water, and how to apply the energy created by the machine to move the vehicle.

The earliest cycle known dates back to 1418. It was called a "manumotive" and was credited to Giovanni Fontana of Padua. It had four wheels and was operated by pulling an endless coil of rope connected to the rear wheels. Near the end of the seventeenth century, a Frenchman, Elie Richard, developed a carriage that called for the passenger to sit up front and steer while his servant operated a treadle in the rear which turned the wheels.

Meanwhile, in 1623, a brilliant Jesuit priest, astronomer and missionary in charge of the Peking observatory, Ferdinand Verbiest, had become the first man to use the word "motor." He invented a steam turbine engine and described it this way: "This machine is a motor which makes it possible to bring into motion any apparatus to which it is attached."

Another early engineer suggested in 1690 that a self-propelled bicycle could be made to go with gunpowder. He was onto something, as rocket pioneer Robert Hutchings Goddard would prove little more than two hundred years later.

Another transportation pioneer wrote in 1784 of his idea to create a piston engine that would make use of air and turpentine that had been placed in contact with a hot surface so it would vaporize and ignite. More than 100 years later, the most advanced motorcycles were still using this "hot tube ignition" principle.

Steam, however, was the first motive power to receive wide use on self-propelled cycles. William Murdock built his first three-wheeler in 1781. Twenty years later Richard Trevithick built a three-wheel steamcycle he called "Puffing Devel" and took seven passengers for a ride on it.

Napoleon Bonaparte granted a patent on January 30, 1807, for a "fire engine" to Isaac de Rivaz. De Rivaz's internal combustion engine had already been perfected and in fact had once been destroyed by fire in 1788. A witness to the trial of the Frenchman's motor vehicle in 1804 gave this description: "[It] was not driven through the direct explosion of a gaseous substance, but by a motor that worked by means of those explosions in such a way that the vehicle moved forward in smooth motion and not by starts and jerks."

Not everything invented at the time was a step in the right direction. David Gordon of England invented something he called the "Squirrel Locomotive" engine in 1824. It had artificial horse legs that worked like the legs of a squirrel running inside a cage to make it turn. If that seems amusing, consider the advertisement for a three-wheel vehicle called the Cynophere which appeared in magazines fifty years later in the United States. The Cynophere was powered by two dogs running inside the two rear wheels. This is how it was advertised:

> Invented by M. Huret, of Paris, France, and Patented in the United States, December 14, 1875.
>
> The Cynophere consist of two large wheels, between which is a comfortable seat and rest for the feet. In front is a small guide wheel, the direction being controlled at will by a rod held in the right hand, while at the left is a brake by which the speed is regulated. Power is furnished by a dog within each of the side wheels, and so light is the draft that it is no more exertion for the dogs to run upon the treadway of the wheel than it is to go at the same speed at their own pleasure. The French Society for the Prevention of Cruelty to Animals, to whom the subject was submitted by the inventor, unanimously endorsed the system.
>
> The vehicle is light and graceful in its mechanism, and can be used by ladies and children, as well as gentlemen, without the slightest danger, discomfort or exertion. For pleasure purposes it is unsurpassed, and when fully introduced to the American public is destined to achieve a popularity far greater than that of the velocipede, while the moderate expense will bring it within the easy reach of all.

Imagine trading in the family six-cylinder sedan for a sporty Cynophere and a matched pair of greyhounds!

By the mid-1880s the idea of noisy, smoking, steam-hissing tricycles that frightened livestock and people alike was so offensive to most Britons that adventurous early riders often found themselves the targets of rock-throwers. Feelings grew so strong that soldiers occasionally had to intervene in disputes over steamcycles using the public roads. The result of emotionalism over the early steamcycles was curious indeed. The British people, who were at the forefront of the Industrial Revolution and enjoyed a tremendous technological lead over every other nation in the world, caused a series of laws to be passed that nearly brought development of self-propelled vehicles to a standstill for twenty years. In the late 1850s Parliament put into effect a 4-mile-an-hour national speed limit. The "Locomotives on Highways Act" required each motor vehicle to have three operators and a fourth man who was required to walk in front carrying a red flag to warn others on the road ahead. These laws were stricken from the books years later, but not before they became a laughingstock and were brazenly ignored. But in the meantime, significant motorcycle progress was made in Germany, France and America, while the British saw their advantage slip away.

Joseph Etienne Lenoir was sixteen years old in 1858 when he built a 1½-horsepower gasoline-burning engine. He applied for a patent and received one on January 24, 1860. In 1863 he drove a four-wheel carriage from Paris to Joinville and back, a distance of 18 kilometers, in an hour and a half. The internal combustion engine developed rapidly after that.

In 1862 a Frenchman, Alphonse Beau de Rochas, published a paper describing the operation of the modern four-stroke engine. A working model of the four-stroke was patented in 1876 by Dr. N. A. Otto of Germany. Dr. Otto's development was to have a profound effect on both the motorcycle and automotive industries, because of the influence it had on one of his assistants. He was Gottfried Jellinek, a brash, rebellious young man from a well-to-do family. He soon quit Otto's employ to found the Daimler-Benz Company in Germany, first as a manufacturer of motorized bicycles and later as one of the world's great auto making companies whose products bear the proud tri-star of Mercedes-Benz today.

Meanwhile, the steam-powered bicycle became a reality in America about 1869 when Sylvester H. Roper of Roxbury, Massachusetts, built what he called a velocipede. Fortunately, the three-wheel machine has been preserved by the Smithsonian Institution in Washington, D.C., and can still be seen today. Primitive though it was, it worked. The steam was heated over a vertical fire tube that hung in the center of three wood spoke wheels. Steam rushed out to push a set of two piston rods, which were connected to 2½-

inch cranks on either side of the rear axle. The front wheel, connected to the rear wheels by a wrought iron fork, had a straight handle bar with wooden grips. The operator was supposed to reach down and insert lumps of coal into the fire box through a small round door at the side.

Roper was another whose life was threatened when he took the steamcycle out on the roads near his home. Neighbors had him arrested for frightening their horses, but he was always released by police when he pointed out that there was no law on the books forbidding the operation of his machine. Townspeople lobbied with the city council and got an ordinance passed, but it was quickly repealed when the council was reminded it had appropriated $5000 for the development of a steam-powered fire engine.

Sylvester Roper continued building steamcycles through 1896, when he was seventy-two years old. His last model developed a fantastic (for that time) 8 horsepower, and carried him at speeds up to 40 mph. So proud was he of his motorbike that Roper entered a local bicycle race and left the others behind in a trail of soot and smoke the first lap around the one-mile track. As he began the second lap, the steamcycle wavered and crashed. Officials reported later that he had apparently died of a heart attack.

Just before Roper built his first steamcycle in 1869, a Frenchman named Michel was credited with developing a velocipede powered by steam called the "Bone Shaker." It had a one-cylinder engine driving the rear wheel. J. H. Knight of Farnham, England, built a steam tricycle in 1874, but he didn't get around to making another one for twenty years. Sir Thomas Parkyns built a steam tricycle in 1881, exhibited it at a London cycle show and received several orders from prospective buyers. Another Englishman named Meek built a steam three-wheeler in 1887.

In Philadelphia, the enterprising Lucius Copeland began adding steam engines to bicycles and selling them. He had invented a steam engine with a condenser on it in 1884. The condenser converted steam back to water and thus stretched the range of the motorcycle. It was quite a revolutionary idea for its day, since almost all steam engines were "open" and merely dissipated steam into the air. This required that they stop frequently to fill up with water. The condenser gave Copeland a silent one-half horsepower motor that emitted no smoke or visible steam while scooting him along at 12 mph. He went to Arizona, California, and finally New York before finding backers for his steamcycle. He opened a plant under the name of Northrup Manufacturing Company and produced two hundred bikes.

Count Albert De Dion, a distinguished sportsman and pioneer of both the motorcycle and automobile industries, built his first steam tricycle in 1884. Seven years earlier, the famous champion of steam cars, France's Leon Serpollet, had built a three-wheel steamer, but it wasn't until 1889 that he made history when he drove a friend from Paris to Lyon in it. In 1879 George A. Long of Northfield, Massachusetts, built a steam engine, which he mated the next year with a frame and running gear to be the prototype of the Columbia steam bicycle made for the Weed Sewing Machine Company of Hartford, Connecticut. His patent for a "steam road vehicle" was granted on July 10, 1883. Long's contraption was a reverse tricycle with the single driving wheel in the rear and two spindly wheels up front. It took two people to operate it safely. The Long Steam Tricycle on display at the Smithsonian is believed to be his original effort.

The first gasoline-driven motorcycle was either the work of Gottlieb Daimler in Germany, Edward Butler in England or De Dion in France. Of the three, Daimler is generally considered to be the father of the modern motorcycle for the invention of his incredibly crude and unwieldy two-wheeler.

As we pointed out before, inventing the engine solved only one-fourth of the problem. A motor for a self-propelled vehicle had to be small and light. It needed an economic fuel supply that could be carried with it. And it needed some mechanism to connect it with the wheels on the ground. Most internal combustion motors of the day were connected to a stationary fuel supply and could not be used. Sparking had been tried, but storage batteries necessary to provide electricity were too large and heavy to be practical on a motorcycle. So Daimler had to devise a method for igniting the gasoline inside the combustion chamber of his single-cylinder engine.

What he decided to do after "endless tests and unremitting pursuit of the objective," as he put it, was to pass the gasoline vapor over a hot metal surface while forcing air into the chamber. To do this Daimler inserted a thin tube into the cylinder, and at the bottom of the tube, outside the cylinder, he lighted a Bunsen burner. The flame turned the tube red hot, and the heat was transferred into the chamber by conductivity. It was quite an ingenious scheme, but its reliability and safety left something to be desired. Today it might be described as giving the engine a "hot foot" to make it go.

The Daimler motorcycle also had outside support wheels, which could be likened to the training wheels of today's bicycles except that they could be raised at will, and a tiller for a steering mechanism which was not all that different from the handlebars found on later motorcycles, bicycles, and tricycles.

The first person to test Daimler's two-wheel machine was his son, Paul, who rode it 3 kilometers from the factory in Cannstatt to Unterturkheim. The trip was uneventful, but a short time later Daimler's nephew, Otto Zels, stole the motorcycle for a joy ride and had a hair-raising experience.

Young Zels had watched his cousin light the Bunsen burner and studied how to crank the engine over with the right side of the crankshaft. He pulled back on the control handle, which engaged the clutch and tightened the belt drive. All that he had seen before, and so he knew the operation up to that point. What he didn't know was how to apply the brake, and it didn't occur to Otto that he didn't possess this vital bit of information until he came to a downhill run and began picking up speed.

At the bottom of the hill was a wide curve leading into a narrow street. He steered the motorcycle over to a fence and, like the Grand National stock car driver does today, tried to lean into the wall and scrub away speed. Alas, all he did was scrape his arm. Ahead of him, to his horror, was a horse-drawn cab virtually blocking the entrance to the narrow street. The cab driver had seen him coming, had panicked and stopped right where he could not be avoided. At the last minute the cabby came to and realized he should try to move out of the way, but it was too late.

On impact Zels was thrown headlong over the horse, but fortunately he was unhurt, flipping completely over and landing on his feet. To keep the cab driver quiet, for he was guilty of riding the motorcycle without the owner's permission or knowledge, Zels paid for damages and gave the cabby a sizable tip. In an awkward sense, he had just made history. Zels had survived the first known traffic collision on a motorcycle and paid the first recorded out-of-court settlement. He was also the first man in history ever known to steal a motorcycle.

Motorcycles of the Englishman, Butler, and De Dion in France were built about the same time. De Dion was said to complete his first three-wheel lightweight in 1884, and Butler to invent and patent the gasoline-burning tricycle the same year. However, it took Butler until 1887 to build his cycle, which had two wheels in front.

In 1892 J. D. Roots of England built the first tricycle powered by a two-stroke one-cycle engine, a motor which was invented in 1881 by Sir Dugald Clark. It was ingeniously cooled by water which flowed to the engine through the tubes of the frame. By 1894, Darracq, the famous early French auto manufacturer, began producing and selling the Millet motorcycle. The first four-cylinder motorcycle was produced in 1896 by Colonel H. C. Holden of Great Britain.

One of the most interesting early motorcycles was invented by Louis S. Clarke of Pittsburgh, founder of the Pittsburgh Motor Vehicle Company, later to be known as the Autocar Company. In 1897 he built an experimental three-wheel carriage to gain the experience he believed he needed to produce automobiles. His gasoline engine drove the two rear wheels. There was no throttle. He controlled the speed by use of a spark arrester. The fuel tank was located under the saddle, where it is found in most models today.

In the years immediately preceding the twentieth century, the motorcycle industry had its share of get-rich-quick speculators, as did the auto industry. Many of the pioneers were quick-thinking promoters who had the vision to take chances at the brink of new technology, to jump in where more conservative businessmen dared not set foot. At the same time, there were those conniving money hustlers who were just as anxious to ride the motorized bandwagon by preying on the gullible and excited public.

In 1896 an American promoter, E. J. Pennington, arrived in

Various views of action at a typical motorcycle recreation park,
Indian Dunes Park, near Castaic,
California. Racing and spectator
areas are separated by permanent fencing, and some of the
riding courses are used by both
motorcycles and dune buggies.
Also separated are riding trails
and competition tracks, to enhance safety.

England to make and sell his motorcycles. One of his early proto-types got airborne during a test, and it gave him an idea that would make his product the most talked about motor vehicle in England during the months to come. He commissioned an illustrator to draw a poster which showed the Pennington Motor Bicycle sailing over a river, frightening a number of observers, including two men in a rowboat directly under the cycle. The inspiration for this drawing, which appeared in an extravagant advertising campaign, was said to be the accidental discovery that a motorcycle can actually fly for some distance through the air. Pennington himself claimed it had flown a distance of 65 feet. This, it may be noted, occurred some six years before the Wright brothers actually did fly at Kitty Hawk, North Carolina.

Pennington bikes operated at a minimum speed of 8 mph, a top speed of 30, and were regularly demonstrated at the Coventry bicycle track. Before he could get the motorcycle into production, Pennington sold his patents to another speculator, Harry John Lawson, for 100,000 pounds sterling. Shortly afterward, however, the press, which had faithfully recorded all the wild claims of the inventor, became disenchanted with Pennington. An exposé of his operation ruined him, and all of his companies collapsed.

The 1890s was a decade of rapid engineering progress. The motorcycle, automobile and bicycle industries all benefited from the 1888 invention of the pneumatic tire by John Boyd Dunlop. The inflated tire was in general use by 1895, a year when the De Dion engine replaced its "hot tube" ignition system with electrical works. Widely copied by other engine designers, the one-half horsepower single-cylinder De Dion engine was the standard of the industry. By 1894, the German firm of Hildebrand and Wolfmüller were also commercially producing a gasoline-powered motorcycle in Munich. In 1896 Great Britain's Parliament passed the so-called Emancipation Act, which removed the last of the unreasonable restrictions against motor vehicles and raised the national speed limit to 12 mph. A historic motorcycle race held in England soon afterward was named in honor of the Emancipation Act.

Harry Lawson, the entrepreneur who had paid so much for patent rights to the Pennington motorcycle, had anticipated repeal of his country's ridiculous anti-motor vehicle laws and had begun to purchase patents, licenses and rights to every seemingly worthwhile invention he could get his hands on. One of his acquisitions was the De Dion engine, which he made for various motorcycles he produced under the banner of British Motor Syndicate. Lawson's companies made and sold the Accles, Beeston (King George V helped to popularize motorcycles by riding one on January 28, 1898, while he was still the Duke of York.), Humbers and Bollee. Lawson had created a sort of British General Motors, and he produced not only motorcycles but automobiles (that came out of factories known as the Great Horseless Carriage Company), and Daimlers. He also produced the first auto show in 1896. Ironically, all of these companies went out of business in a very few years, but Lawson is remembered today as the founder of the motor vehicle industry in England.

If any predictions can be made about a motorized vehicle, it is that man will find a way to race it and a way to make war with it. The first motorcycle race of international significance was that Emancipation Run in England in 1896. By 1899 the Simms "Motor Scout" was in action in the South African Boer War. The Simms had four wheels, carried a Maxim gun and 1000 rounds of ammunition. It had a fuel range of 120 miles and was used by dispatch riders.

Beginning in 1897 many motorcycle engines were "clip-ons," which could be affixed to a bicycle, either in front or in back of the rider. The motors rode high, were inconvenient, made for an uncomfortable ride and adversely affected either the weight distribution or the center of gravity or both. The best clip-on engines were made by Menerva of Belgium and Werner of France. Werner clip-ons were found on such early British motorcycles as the Enfield, Quadrant and Triumph. In 1901 the Russian-born Werner brothers built in France the first engine that was an integral part of the bike. Off dropped the bicycle pedals, and the motorcycle began to take on that distinctive appearance it retains today. The Werner, of course, was widely copied.

The Werner featured a spray carburetor. Lubrication was accomplished by means of a hand pump. Riders of Werner-powered cycles learned the tricky art of judging when to pump the oil. On a flat surface they would pump every few miles, more often if the cycle were climbing a hill and had to work harder. Some very astute riders learned to figure when the oil needed pumping by the amount of blue haze in the exhaust smoke or by the feel of the engine. They could feel the engine tighten just before it was about to seize due to oil starvation. Another innovation of the Werner was the foot pedal that operated the rear brake, and the brake, which was nothing more than a block of fiber that pressed against the rim of the wheel. This type of brake was common for the first twenty years of this century. Slides were common on the Werner, because there was no neutral, and when the wheel locked up, the engine stalled.

American motorcycle history, except for those early artifacts mentioned already in this chapter, really began in 1900 with the meeting between bicycle manufacturer George Hendee and mechanic Oscar Hedstrom.

Hedstrom worked on one of the pacer motorcycles that were used by bicycle racers in Madison Square Garden and other bike tracks of the day. A pacer was a motorcycle with a broad plank on the back that was used to cut wind resistance and create a vacuum so the bike rider could travel fast more easily. In fact, bike riders were actually drafting on the motorcycles, having learned the secrets of aerodynamics in racing through their sense of feel—the pressure of wind against their bodies.

Because of the nature of their work, pacer motorcycles had to last for long distances. They needed to be trouble-free. Sitting in Madison Square Garden one night watching the races, the thought occurred to Hendee that a man who could build a reliable pacer might be the ideal person to develop a reliable motorcycle that could be sold to the public. After a race in December 1900, the two men met, and Hendee asked Hedstrom if he thought he could build such a machine. Hedstrom, of course, said yes. They wrote a contract agreement on the back of an old envelope Hendee had been carrying in his pocket, and both men signed it. The American motorcycle industry was born.

Hedstrom went to his home in Middletown, Connecticut, and began design work on the first successful American machine. The following spring his prototype was built and ready for testing. Hedstrom had already tested the bike near his home, but the final trial was to take place at the bicycle factory in Springfield, Massachusetts. A large crowd of curious spectators lined Cross Street hill, which had a 19 percent grade. Hedstrom started at slow speed and accelerated up the hill without a hitch. He deliberately slowed down at the steepest place on the hill, practically stalling the engine, then opened the throttle to demonstrate the reserve power his machine possessed.

A delighted George Hendee immediately leased loft space and began to manufacture the motorcycle, which carried one of the most distinguished names the industry has ever known. The Hendee motorcycle was called the Indian, in honor of the noble Redman who was the true pioneer of America.

Considering the modern trend toward lightweight bikes with high compression engines, the 1901 Indian was years ahead of its time. Weighing only 98 pounds, it had a 1¾-horsepower engine that gave it good acceleration, instant response and a wide speed range. Only three machines were made that year, but production really got under way in 1902, when 143 Indians came off the assembly line.

Hedstrom, who had been a bicycle racer before he began building pacer motorcycles, urged that the Hendee Manufacturing Company plunge into racing to advertise its product. On May 30, 1902, Indian won the Ft. George hillclimb in Bronx, New York, and on July 1–3 of that year George Hendee, Oscar Hedstrom and a Springfield dealer, George Holden, finished first-second-third in the 250-mile New York-to-Boston run, the first marathon race ever held in this country.

About the time the first Indian prototype was being assembled in Oscar Hedstrom's garage, two friends got together with an idea in Milwaukee, Wisconsin. Their idea was to take the hard work out of bicycling. Bill Harley worked as a draftsman by day, and Arthur Davidson was a pattern maker. On their own time, with the aid of a German draftsman who knew about European motorcycles and had a working understanding of the De Dion engine, they tinkered.

Soon they acquired more help. Art's brother, Walter Davidson, was persuaded to join the project. Walter was a skilled mechanic working as a railroad machinist in Parsons, Kansas. Then came

William, a toolmaker, and they had to move their operations to a small shop owned by a friend. Another volunteer who contributed his ideas to the building of that first Harley-Davidson motorcycle was Ole Evinrude, who later became famous in the small craft industry as the originator of the outboard motor bearing his name.

The original Harley-Davidson had a 3-horsepower engine, very powerful for its day, but the partners found that when they tried to climb a steep hill they still had to help it along with their feet. They had started the project with the idea of taking the hard work out of bicycling, so they decided the motor needed to be more powerful, and they went back to work increasing the piston displacement to get more horsepower output.

Harley and the Davidson boys found they were once again running out of room. William C. Davidson, the boys' father, was a cabinetmaker. He built a 10- by 15-foot building in his back yard so they could continue work. The boys hung a sign over the door when it was finished: "Harley-Davidson Motor Company."

The first three Harley-Davidson motorcycles were sold before they were assembled in 1903. A man named Miller bought the first one completed. He rode it for 6000 miles and sold it to a George Lyon who rode it another 15,000 miles before selling it to a Dr. Webster. He added 19,000 miles, sold it to Louis Fluke who rode it 12,000 miles. The machine was last known to be owned by a Stephen Sparrow who put 32,000 miles on it.

The small company grew slowly, increasing production to five motorcycles in 1904 and to eight in 1905. The shed in the Davidsons' back yard had grown to four times its size, but it was overrun with cycle parts. A factory site had to be found.

Securing property on the site of the present factory, the boys framed up a building 28 by 80 feet alongside a railroad spur. Rail employees thought it was too close to the tracks, went to the trouble of surveying the area and proved they were right. So the Davidsons got together a gang of eight or ten husky young fellows, picked up the framework of the shop and moved it back a foot and a half.

Like all growing young firms, Harley-Davidson needed capital. In the early 1900s it wasn't too easy to walk into your neighborhood bank and say, "Hi there. I'm making a great new product called a motorcycle, and I'm interested in a loan." But the company did survive that difficult period quite easily. The resourceful Davidson boys went to an uncle in Madison, Wisconsin, who they knew had enough capital, and borrowed it from him. Because he was a beekeeper, they called him their "honey uncle."

In the final analysis, the success of any manufacturing company depends upon the quality of its products. At the time Indian and Harley-Davidson were only two companies in an industry that became quite crowded early in this century. One of those early companies was Reading-Standard, which boasted in its advertising "Manufactured and tested in the mountains." One wiseacre added, "Tested in the mountains, all right. It must have been tested downhill."

Other early competitors were Orient, Wagner, Rambler, Dyke, Tribune, Steffey, Yale, Auto-Bi, Columbia, Shaw, Curtiss (the aircraft company founded by aviation pioneer Glenn Curtiss), Duck, Pope, Mitchell, Greer, Holley, Minneapolis, Marathon Marsh, Merkel and Miami. A company which made one of the classic motorcycles was Excelsior, founded in 1911. It lasted twenty-one years but fell victim to the Great Depression.

Motorcycle companies here and abroad prospered in the years between 1900 and the start of World War I, when many of their important engineering advances were made. Motorcycles truly improved from year to year, but their prospects for survival during the greatest transportation revolution the world has ever known were poor indeed. Motorcycles were sold in those early years as basic transportation, and as such they could not compete against the automobile.

During this exciting period, 1900–1915, rawhide and leather drive belts were replaced by chains, the magneto was adopted, the sprung front fork and kick starter were invented, a three-speed gearbox was tried and so was a variable speed transmission. The 1914 Indian Twin used an electrical system which ran the lights as well as the ignition system, eliminating the bothersome gas lamp.

Accelerating the engineering advances of the period and the popularity of motorcycle racing everywhere was the advent of the Isle of Man Tourist Trophy, the world's most important motorcycle race. But as suddenly as the motorcycle boom began in the burst of engineering creativity at the start of the century, it died with the start of World War I. Twenty-five makes of American motorcycles disappeared from the scene between 1915 and 1917.

World War I marked the first time in history when broad use of motorcycles was made by military forces. Triumph produced 30,000 motorbikes for the British army, and the American Expeditionary Force had 10,000 motorcycles, mostly Indians. NSU made a lightweight machine for the Kaiser's army. It's interesting to note that armies have made less and less use of motorcycles since then. The U.S. Army had an inventory of about 5500 bikes at the start of World War II. This figure had dropped to about 1000 by the mid-1950s, when they were used almost exclusively for traffic control. In Vietnam during 1969, a reconaissance unit of the 25th Infantry actually introduced motorcycles to combat as an experiment! Officers were surprised to find the recon riders could cover three times as much ground in a day as a foot soldier, and they were pleased to discover motorcycles were very effective on the narrow bicycle trails used by Viet Cong supply personnel. The VC, on the other hand, also knew the value of motorcycles in their terrorist activities. The throwing of grenades and bombs from motorcycles became such a problem in Saigon that authorities made it mandatory for a motorcycle passenger to ride sidesaddle. That way, they reasoned, it would be more difficult to hide a bomb, and the passenger would find it more difficult to balance himself. Thus, he would be hampered from throwing a deadly missile or firing a weapon.

In World War II, during the Normandy invasion, the British battleship H.M.S. *Rodney* stood offshore lobbing in shells at the direction of a spotter plane. After knocking out all the important targets, the pilot continued to direct only one of the ship's nine 16-inch guns. Each time the battleship fired, the pilot would radio back, "Up a thousand." After several rounds, each one fired 1000 yards farther inland, the ship's gunnery officer became curious and inquired what was the target at which he was firing.

"A dirty Hun, sir," came the reply. "He's on a motorbike, and he's heading inland as fast as his two wheels can take him."

It remained for the post-World War II era to produce a revival of interest in the motorcycle, not as a specialized mode of transportation, but rather as a recreation vehicle. Leadership in this development came from one of the world's most unlikely places, Japan.

Japan had been a backward, feudal country which refused to join the outside world and resisted any attempt of others to establish contact until America's Commodore Perry sailed into Tokyo harbor with his gunboats in 1854. The successful Japanese race to catch up with other industrialized nations of the world since that time is well known, but its early ventures into motorcycling were so insignificant that the rest of the world ignored them.

The first motorcycle, a steamer of unknown origin, was imported into Japan in 1899. Narazo Shimazu designed and built the first Japanese motorcycle engine in 1908, and the first company to make a complete motorbike was Miyata in 1913, but Miyata suspended production of its two-wheeler in 1916. A handful of companies were building only 3037 a year in 1940, and in the devastation of war they could assemble only 211 in 1945.

Into this vacuum came a school dropout mechanic who had raced automobiles until a serious accident forced him to quit. In 1947 at the age of forty-one, Soichiro Honda contemplated his hard luck. He had been a successful piston manufacturer, but the Americans had destroyed his factory by bombing. Rather than heap self-pity on himself, he began to look around for a product he could make which would have a market among his countrymen. He hit upon the idea of manufacturing a motorbike, which he started to do by buying five hundred war surplus generators and attaching them to bicycles. Pretty soon he had sold all five hundred and there were no more generators to buy. So he designed his own motorcycle.

Honda launched his business in two board shacks in a bomb-shattered district of Hammamatsu with thirty-four employees and $2777 in the bank. Weathering one financial crisis after another (Japan has business recessions, too), Honda built a business that has meant a world-wide boom to the motorcycle industry and has been the backbone of Japan's postwar export expansion.

Today's motorcycle bears quite a resemblance to its early antecedents. A fellow who travels in Europe every summer visited a

The basic design of motorcycles hasn't changed much in half a century, as can be seen from this view of a 1919 Cleveland.

museum in England, where several examples of early motorbikes are on exhibit along with the later, more exotic products of the country's well-respected motorcycle technology.

"You know," he said, "I couldn't help thinking that despite all this talk about styling, one motorcycle looked pretty much like every other one."

It's true they all have two wheels, a motor, a seat and handle bars, and it's also true that motorcycles today are vastly different from the two-wheelers of an earlier generation. However, the biggest difference is that motorcycles in today's society have changed their function. No longer must they be depended upon for basic transportation. They are go-anywhere machines that invite the rider to the open road, the countryside, the mountains, the desert.

Today's motorcyclist has a limitless choice of destinations. He can enjoy an infinite variety of riding experiences. For some motorcycle manufacturers, it took half a century to discover what any enthusiast could have told them in a minute—the motorcycle is more than a method of transportation; it's also a fun machine.

2
I'll Have
One of Each

A used-car salesman of our acquaintance once told us there are only three kinds of automobile buyers: One wants to own a particular make of car, one wants to pay a certain amount for his car and the other wants to pay so much a month. The first fellow will walk onto the lot looking for a Ford. He might drive out in a Model A or an LTD; it doesn't matter what year, what it costs or how much mileage is on the odometer. The second buyer has $800 to spend, and he wants an $800 automobile, no matter if it is a foreign sports car, a station wagon, a two-door sedan or a pickup truck. The third fellow, even more poorly advised than the other two, wants to make payments of $65 a month, and he'll buy anything the salesman offers him so long as he can get it on those terms.

Too often the novice motorcycle buyer approaches a showroom without even as much of an idea about what he wants as our three used-car shoppers. The most common mistake of a first-time buyer is to walk in and ask the price of the biggest, most expensive machine in the place. If good motorcycle salesmen were like the car guys, they'd have this fellow's gold fillings out of his mouth in ten minutes.

The big, fast bike has the glamour, the mystique. Possibly it is the machine he first read about in one of the motorcycle magazines which consistently play up the hot performers. In any motorcycle dealership the most publicized machine on display is usually the Ferrari of the line. Fortunately for our unsuspecting buyer, the good dealer or his salesman will ask a few discreet questions about his riding experience and usually try to talk the real amateur down to a smaller, less potentially dangerous machine.

The slightly more sophisticated buyer makes another mistake, going for a machine that isn't adequate to his needs. The reason he does this, according to one top-notch dealer, is that he doesn't think about the "long range usability" of his motorcycle.

"He buys what a friend told him he ought to have or what a salesman sold him on," the dealer said. "He doesn't look ahead a year and a half or two years to see what he is going to do with the bike or whether or not he is going to enjoy it. Most first-time buyers and even many second-time buyers really don't know what they want when they come in the door."

Price sometimes plays a factor in this buyer's choice of machines. He knows that too small a bike isn't legal to ride on the freeway or expressway. So he gets a machine that just barely meets the minimum and then, the dealer said, "goes out and runs it on the freeway and shortens the life of the machine."

Just like the three "marks" of the used-car salesman, the average motorcycle buyer is either swayed by the sex appeal of a big brute machine, is hooked on price, or takes bad advice. He forgets to think for himself about why he is buying a motorcycle and what he wants to do with it after he gets it.

One of the first mistakes the first-time purchaser makes when talking with the salesman is not admitting that he doesn't know how to ride. This is an understandable ego hangup, because it is embarrassing to many people to have to admit they don't know how to do something. The salesman, however, knows right away if he is dealing with an intelligent customer when he hears him speak those difficult words: "I've never ridden one before."

Sammy Tanner, the well-known racer, once sold motorcycles for a dealership in Long Beach, California. One day a man in his forties drove up in a Cadillac with his good-looking girlfriend and began browsing.

After some hesitation the fellow did state he had never ridden a motorcycle before. Noting he was nervous talking about it in front of his pretty female companion, Sammy suggested they retire to a side street so he could get some instruction. The man showed good aptitude and learned quickly the rudiments of handling the motorcycle. After a while his tension vanished, and Sammy thought he was ready to buy. That's when the customer rode the bike back onto the lot where his girlfriend was waiting and apparently decided to show off.

Opening the throttle, he roared down the narrow space between the bikes on display. Suddenly he froze at the controls and couldn't stop, crashing into a row of new machinery, bouncing up onto a display stand and destroying the bike sitting on it. The terrified customer spotted the driveway and tried to aim for it but missed and hit the side of the building next door. The noise brought everybody in the shop out to the lot to aid the victim, who lay somewhat groggy and bleeding on the sidewalk.

"Let's get you to the hospital," Sammy said. "Oh no, I can't go to the hospital," the man insisted. No matter how many argued with him that he should have medical treatment or at least an examination, he stood his ground. He wouldn't go. Finally Sammy asked him why.

"I haven't got the time," the customer said. "I'm on my way down to the unemployment office to collect my check."

Sammy Tanner learned later that the expensive car his "customer" had driven to the agency that day was stolen.

Most salesmen, who are after all working for a commission and

Customer makes close inspection of used motorcycles on a dealer's lot.

are responsible for sales rather than the safety record of the motor-cycle riders of the world, are very good about making sure a customer can handle the equipment he is buying. However, the minute a buyer says he knows how to ride, the salesman will back off and not question him further, because he is interested in making the sale and doesn't want to do anything to discourage it. That's important to remember.

A good salesman, once having made the sale, will give the customer a thorough checkout on controls and the functions of important components of the motorcycle. He will talk about simple maintenance and usually supply the buyer with either the owner's manual or a simple brochure that tells about care and maintenance. At that time he may learn that the customer doesn't know how to ride, and he usually will take time out to give a quick course in basic riding. He's not paid to do that. He is sincerely interested in making sure the customer is happy, because a happy customer is a repeat customer. But theoretically every minute the salesman spends away from the showroom floor is time he could be spending making another sale.

It's also a sad but true statement that fully 50 percent of all motorcycle buyers do not ask for a briefing on the controls. In those cases, it's the well-trained, thoughtful salesman who volunteers the information and refuses to leave the customer alone until he is convinced that the buyer knows what he is doing on the motorcycle.

Despite the good intentions, however, somewhere in the United States today there is probably a new motorcycle owner riding off the dealer's lot, blipping the throttle and sailing into the back of a parked car.

We mentioned earlier "long range usability." One of the most common errors a buyer makes is not knowing what he is going to do with the motorcycle when he buys it. It might help to know just what is available, to know something about sizes, weights, different horsepower and torque characteristics of the available machinery. We'll try to discuss each different type of motorcycle a little later in this chapter.

But first let's examine the price-shopper. There is certainly nothing wrong with touring from one dealership to another to see which offers the best "deal." The average price of a new motorcycle works out to about $600, which usually buys a motorcycle in the 125 to 175cc range. That's a lot of money to commit to anything, particularly for the young man of sixteen to twenty-five who makes up the bulk of the motorcycle market.

The motorcycle retail business is much like the automobile business in this regard. Auto dealers long ago gave up trying to make buyers pay the so-called "list" price. In fact, they have encouraged price chiseling to the extent that manufacturer's suggested prices are almost a fiction today. Shrewd shopping for a motorcycle will likely produce a savings, because motorcycle dealers, like their auto agency cousins, shave prices. A dealer might also reduce or eliminate preparation and destination charges, or offer attractive terms to win the buyer away from his competitors.

Shopping is an accepted practice, but one thing to keep in mind is that after the purchase comes service. A new motorcycle owner would be smart to buy where he expects that service to be performed.

Human nature being what it is, a dealer hates to have a bike purchaser shop his store, go out and buy from another dealer and then come in and expect warranty work and other service privileges. If at all possible, buy from a dealer who has a good service operation. Most warranties are standard contracts calling for a period of ninety days or so when all parts and labor for product failure are to be provided at no cost to the purchaser. Warranties usually extend to one year or 5000 miles, whichever occurs first, and they cover serious failures but not routine servicing. Since warranty work is something that is spelled out not only in the contract between the buyer and the dealer but also between the dealer and the factory distributor, they can be relied on to give the customer what he has coming regardless of what the dealer would like to do. It's a lot more pleasant, however, to have the man caring for your motorcycle sincerely thinking of your best interests.

So how does a buyer select a "good service" dealer, one who will give him courteous treatment, charge him fair prices, do reliable work and sell him quality replacement parts and accessories?

One quick way to tell is to step back into the service department and take a look. Dealerships vary in size from "mom and pop" stores to large establishments employing nearly one hundred people. If the service department has more than a handful of employees, if there is a lot of work in progress with some backlog and if it is neatly laid out and just looks efficient, chances are it's a good service dealership.

On the other hand, if the place is dirty, if only one or two mechanics are on duty, if there is horseplay or obvious malingering going on, if the layout is cramped or sloppy, if tools and testing equipment are not stored neatly, or if there is little backlog of work on the premises, the customer might be hesitant to trust his new machine to this dealer.

The final test, before actually taking a motorcycle in and having it serviced or repaired, is to talk to someone who has had work done there. There is no way for a motorcycle dealer to keep all his customers happy, but it is impossible for him to keep unhappy customers from talking about bad experiences they've had. If

There is a noticeable difference between a street bike (left) and an off-road motorcycle. Note the smooth tire tread on the street version, compared with the knobby-type tire at right. Although motorcycle tires are round, not flat, street treads are more like automobile tire treads. A long street saddle gives comfort to two riders, while an off-road motorcycle typically carries only one person. The easiest detail to spot is the placement of the exhaust pipe. It is low and below the rider's feet on a street machine and high on the off-road bike to avoid rocks and water.

someone you know was not satisfied with the dealer in question, he'll surely talk about it.

An important factor in the selection of a motorcycle that is frequently overlooked by the buyer—but hardly ever by the good salesman—is size.

A good rule of thumb for the first-time owner is that he is better off with a machine that is close to his own weight and has a comfortable wheelbase. The fellow who is 5 feet 4 inches tall and weighs 140 pounds would have a difficult time wrestling with anything heavier than 250 pounds. On the other hand, the 6-foot 2-inch 225-pounder needs the long wheelbase of a larger machine to keep from cramping his legs, and he certainly should be big enough to handle the extra weight of a big bike.

It is a bit much to expect women, who generally weigh between 100 and 125 pounds to be comfortable handling anything over 150 pounds.

In the process of analyzing what kind of motorcycle to buy, the beginner could do worse than talk with experienced motorcycle riders. They've made the mistakes already, and like all enthusiasts and hobbyists they are happy to talk about their equipment and the riding enjoyment they get. Motorcyclists are not hard to find. There may be one in the neighborhood. They are found in school and office parking lots. They are likely to go to motorcycle races, go camping in resort areas and attend club events in nearly every community. A list of clubs, their addresses and their events are often found on the newsstands in weekly publications like *Cycle News* and *Motorcycle Weekly*.

What the beginning rider should learn quickly is that there are two basic kinds of motorcycles, those for the street and those for off-the-road riding. Although some machines are adaptable to both, most models fall into one category or the other. There are several types of street machines, off-road bikes and so-called street scramblers. Let's take a look at some of them:

MOTORCYCLES FOR THE STREET

These are primarily designed for enjoyment on the open road, but the latest models are on their good behavior in low speed,

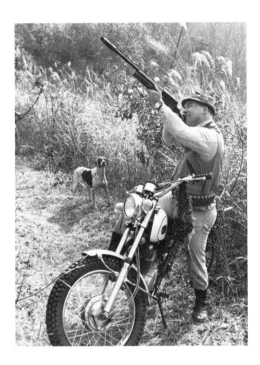

A hunter demonstrates typical off-road use of a trail bike. Note the bird which is slung from the handle bar.

stop-and-go conditions found in crowded cities as well. Street bikes are likely to have two cylinders instead of one, come equipped with a longer seat so two people can ride, carry larger fuel tanks and have tires with a normal tread design. Exhaust pipes travel from the motor underneath the feet and straight back. Engines of most models are designed so that the motorcycle can hum along at the speed limit effortlessly with lots of power to spare.

Manufacturers offer a number of comfort-oriented accessories, such as fairings to break the wind, buddy seats, handgrips, back rests, windshields and even radios. They also offer such cross-country touring gear as saddlebags and luggage racks.

All street bikes are not large, heavy honkers, but come in engine power choices down to the minimum horsepower required for use on freeways and expressways (some with even fewer horses) and to total weight of less than 150 pounds.

The American manufacturer Harley-Davidson is generally associated with bulky 500-pound machines that require a muscular giant to push up the street, but Harley offers handsome 65, 125 and 350cc models that weigh from 140 to 259 pounds. Japanese manufacturers have a variety of street machinery that runs the entire range of engine size from 50 to 750cc (4½ to 67 horse-power), and several British makes are world-famous for the high quality of their road bikes. Except for Bridgestone, which makes street bikes as small as 100cc of piston displacement (11 horse-power), the Anglo tradition runs to larger, long-range touring bikes.

A confirmed honker enthusiast might argue the point, but if the beginning rider intends doing much traveling in heavy traffic, he might be better off shopping for one of the lighter, less powerful machines. Coming to a legal stop and putting the foot down is a lot easier when the bike weighs 250 to 300 pounds than when it hefts a solid 700 pounds of steel, plastic and rubber. The smaller the engine, however, the slower the cruising speed, and the less comfortable a rider is likely to feel in the fast lane.

For any beginning motorcyclist, and for most experienced off-road riders as well, the purchase of a street bike should be approached very carefully and thoughtfully.

MOTORCYCLES FOR OFF-THE-ROAD

The off-road bike has a different job to perform, and therefore, it is engineered quite differently. The gearing is close ratio, and the power curve extends upward to the highest engine speeds, but it is notable for good low end torque that gives quick acceleration at low speeds. That is what is needed in the rough and tumble environment for which it is built.

It's easy to tell an off-road machine from a street bike by looking at the tires. Dirt bike tires have knobs one-half inch square in place of the street tread. The exhaust pipe is also a dead giveaway. It slants upward from the header and passes under the fuel tank and seat.

Look closer at the off-road machine, and other factors show up. The frame is light—the largest desert racing machines weigh in under 250 pounds—and there is also invariably only a one-cylinder engine. The suspension is sprung more loosely. The front fork has a five-inch travel or more, and the rear shocks have two to four inches of give. Engine sizes, and thus horsepower potential, run

Dragster bikes, like this Harley-Davidson twin, cover the quarter-mile in less than 9 seconds and hit speeds over 170 mph while the rider wiggles back and forth, partly to achieve balance and partly to apply more weight to the rear wheel for better traction. Note that the frame is specially built and is much longer than a stock motorcycle frame.

the gamut from 50 to 500cc depending on the specialized use for which the machine is built. And there are several uses.

Sportsmen have created a demand for a go-anywhere bike that can be used to reach remote hunting and fishing sites. This type of conveyance is also rugged and powerful enough to haul back such game as deer, elk and bear. So-called trail bikes are good for climbing, although they are not designed for speed, even on the flat. They are useful for herding livestock, and the U.S. Forest Service has been experimenting with their use on fire trails for years. Another breed of motorcycle enthusiast prefers the trail bike, the trail explorer. In this group are people who don't particularly enjoy dashing about like a jackrabbit over rocks and gullies but merely like to ride up trails to see what is at the other end. Many geologists and nature lovers are in this group. They find pleasure putt-putting about in the wilderness, taking in the sights or collecting specimens.

The street scrambler is used about nine-tenths of the time on the street, but is adaptable to the dirt. It is heavier than the usual off-road machine and is therefore a little more difficult to handle over rough terrain. A scrambler owner can easily learn to change wheels and make rear shock adjustments to improve the handling when switching from the asphalt surface to dirt or back again.

A special kind of non-racing competition, trials riding, has developed a completely different breed of off-road bike, the trials machine. The object of trials is to cover a terribly difficult obstacle course without removing the feet from the footpegs. Each touch-down is called a "dab" and is counted against the rider. The toughest trials include water hazards as well as a diabolically conceived series of dirt, sand, mud and rock obstructions. The favorite trick of the people who lay out trials courses is to find a fallen log that is three feet or more in diameter and guide the course over that seemingly impossible obstacle. Good trials riders clear such logs with ease. The trials machine has a small fuel tank and very small footpegs, which are miniaturized to prevent their striking the ground. The trials engine is built for strong low end torque but with no necessity for a high top speed, since trials riding is done mostly between 10 and 20 mph.

THE RACING BIKE

A friend of ours refused to buy his teen-age son a motorcycle to ride back and forth to school because he said it was too dangerous, but he did get him a racing bike.

"I don't worry about him on the race track," the man said. "The riders are all excellent, they are going in the same direction and there are no 4000 pound automobiles to run into."

This isn't a recommendation to start the youngster out on a racing bike, but it might be a good thing to know something about competition machinery. Racers come in all sizes, from 50cc to 1000. There are even mini-bike races with no age limit. Racing is as diversified as pleasure riding, and a variety of frames, suspension systems, gearing and engines are available for most makes of motorcycles which produce racing models.

The classic machine is the road racer, which started out in development half a century ago as a street machine and evolved from there. Engines are exotic and tuned to the most precise settings possible. Handlebars are the small clip-on type. They feature huge brakes, either drum or disc, and they have larger than normal fuel tanks, usually about five gallons. The frame is very light, the steering is lightning fast, and the rider crouches behind a streamlined fairing that often has been designed in a wind tunnel for maximum aerodynamic efficiency.

On the dirt ovals are found the Class C flat track bikes, which are light but extremely rugged motorcycles with specified engine sizes that are designed to turn primarily in one direction, to the left. Normally they have four-stroke engines and weigh about 200 pounds. In 1971 the rule forbidding use of brakes was rescinded, and by the end of the season about half of the touring pros had disc brakes on the rear wheel. Flat track bikes also feature a quick-change rear axle to allow for rapid sprocket and wheel swaps to adjust to local track conditions. A specialized type of dirt track racer is the Class A speedway bike, which has a superlight rigid frame weighing less than the motorcycle engine and a fuel-burning 500cc motor that is only good for sprints of less than two miles of racing at one time.

The TT (Tourist Trophy) motorcycle is designed specifically to turn left and right on a dirt course that meanders in tight curls and has a jump to negotiate. There are strong disc brakes front and rear, and the engine is built with lots of low end torque and horse-power.

As for the ultimate dirt racing bike, it is the moto-cross racer. It is tough, reliable, extremely well balanced and light. It is likely to have a 21-inch front wheel in place of the stock 19-inch front wheel and huge brakes front and rear. Motocross bikes are also very light, weighing 230 pounds or less.

Slightly different, but built much the same, is the desert racing machine, which campaigns in such events as the Mint 400 and the Baja 1000. Because it travels longer without stopping, it has a larger fuel capacity than a moto-cross bike, and because it is designed to run at 70 to 80 mph over incredibly rough terrain and to handle well in the loose dirt and sand; it has a 19-inch wheel.

One more type of competition machine remains, the drag bike, which is designed for one purpose only, to cover the quarter-mile in the shortest possible time. It is usually homemade to the lightest possible specification, including replacement of steel with such exotic metals as titanium, vanadium and aluminum. Usually all-out drag bikes have two or three engines, either mounted one behind the other or side by side. The rear tire has a flat surface like an automobile tire. The handlebars are clip-ons, and the seat is usually a sheet of aluminum the rider lies across, wiggling his weight back and forth, partly to stay upright and partly to force more weight to the rear wheel to improve the traction. A half-gallon tank carries either gasoline or nitromethane, depending on what class the motorcycle is competing in.

WHAT ABOUT ENGINE SIZES?

By automobile standards motorcycles have tiny engines, but they also make possible fantastic power-to-weight ratios by comparison. This power-to-weight superiority is what makes motorcycles such exciting performers.

Let's compare the American pony car's V8 horsepower of 250 with its 3000 pounds of weight to a street 250cc (16-cubic-inch) motorcycle putting out 25 horsepower and weighing 220 pounds. The car has about a 1–to–12 power-to-weight ratio, while the ratio for the motorcycle is about 1–to–9. That's a dramatic difference.

Piston displacement in motorcycles and automobiles can be compared in the same way a thimble might be set up alongside a water glass. The size differences are so great that it is impractical to translate motorcycle piston displacement into the cubic inches listed for American automobiles. Nearly all motorcycle engines are measured in cubic centimeters, from the smallest 50cc motorbikes and minicycles to the 1200cc kings of the road. To make a comparison, simply remember that 1 cubic inch is equal to 16.387 cubic centimeters. To put it another way, 1000cc or 1 liter is equal to 61.025 cubic inches. It would take the displacement of twenty Harley 250s to equal that of one Mustang 305-cubic-inch V8.

It is generally, but often incorrectly, thought that the more inexperienced the rider, the smaller the engine he should have at his disposal. On the contrary, the 50cc engine with a slow throttle response takes a great deal of skill to master, since a motorcycle becomes more and more stable as it increases speed. Manipulating a small bike requires good concentration and co-ordination to keep it constantly in the most efficient driving gear. On the other hand, a beginning rider is courting trouble if he climbs on a big engine monster and roars down the highway.

Like most good things in life, moderation in the selection of a motorcycle engine is the best course to follow. The middle range is hard to beat, 125 to 250cc.

THE HELMET AND OTHER ACCESSORIES

A new motorcycle may cost anywhere from $400 to $2500, but every smart rider knows the next $20 to $50 he spends is the most important cash outlay he will make. That is the cost of a reliable safety helmet. Some states require the use of helmets, but it shouldn't matter if they do or not. The helmet covers the most vital area of the body, the part we think, see, talk, hear, eat and smell with, and the part that is the most vulnerable to severe and even fatal injury.

We use the term "reliable" rather than "approved," because there is some current controversy over so-called "approved" helmets. Every safety helmet sold in a motorcycle shop meets a voluntary standard set by the American National Standard Institute known as Z90. The controversy exists over policing, as there are claims that some manufacturers do not maintain the high Z90 standard after having attained it and passed the initial test. The industry itself has moved to correct this oversight by forming a group called the Safety Helmet Council Association that plans to enforce the proper labeling of Z90 approved helmets.

Meanwhile, such a distinguished journalist as Ivan Wagar, editor of *Cycle World*, has reported that Z90 approved helmets have been taken out of shipping crates fresh from the factory with cracks in them or have been damaged merely by falling off the showroom shelf. That's hardly good enough performance to make you want to entrust a human skull to one of those brain buckets. The SNELL 1970 standard is more rigorous than Z90. Several companies, including Bell & H.A. make helmets which meet this standard.

The most reliable material used in the manufacture of a helmet is fiberglass, and it might be wise to stick to it until the controversy has been resolved. The questionable material at this point is an injection molded polycarbonate, which under normal conditions would be hard as a rock, and would probably exceed fiberglass for toughness.

An essential in motorcycle safety is a helmet. A large percentage of motorcycle accidents result in head injuries when helmets are not worn, and head injuries can be serious and sometimes fatal. Rider (top, left) displays a typical helmet and also wears protective glasses. Rider (top, right) also wears a helmet but carries with him dark goggles for day wear and clear goggles for night riding. A woman rider (left) puts on a different type of helmet, which covers less of her neck and face.

However, polycarbonate is susceptible to cracking when exposed to solvents, gasoline and a number of other substances and it requires some caution in handling, cleaning and storing to prevent damage.

Helmets are available in a number of designs. Some helmets cover only the cranium, ending at a line just above ear level. Most of them cover the ears and the neck. The best is said to offer full face protection. It has a strip which joins the left and right sides of

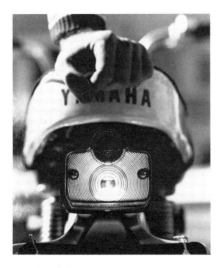

Location of the stoplight, tail-light and reflector, essentials to all properly equipped motorcycles. Wise, safety conscious riders check their stop and tail-lights regularly.

the headpiece just below the nose, effectively covering the mouth and chin.

Just as vital as head protection is eye protection. It is up to the rider to decide which of two types of eye coverings he prefers and then to use one of them every time he rides. Goggles, which can cost less than a dollar to as much as $10, are the usual means of covering the eyes. They should be made of plastic rather than glass, to prevent splintering on impact of some foreign object, which inevitably implants small glass fragments in the eye.

Most helmets are offered with a button-on option, the plastic face shield. These are particularly recommended to a rider who must wear prescription glasses. Face shields are available in clear or tinted plastic, giving the rider the option of wearing a tinted shield to cut down glare during the daytime or a clear shield for night riding.

Gloves are recommended for the same reason eye protection is strongly suggested. A large bug, a stone or other object may fly at a motorcyclist at any time, and a surprise stinging blow could easily cause the rider to take his hand off the handlebars at precisely the wrong moment, causing a serious accident.

It should hardly be necessary to advise a motorcyclist against going barefoot or wearing tennis shoes, but it is surprising how many riders risk broken feet, sprained ankles and worse by ignoring the simple reality that the ground is harder than the human foot, and it is frequently pockmarked with holes to snag an unsuspecting toe. Footwear should be leather, and lace-up boots are strongly recommended for off-road use, as well as being required for racing. Why lace-up boots? Try taking off a pull-over boot over a swollen, sprained ankle sometime.

For street riding a must option is the rearview mirror. It is difficult to use effectively on a motorcycle, but it is not only required for street licensing, their use on a motorcycle is even more protection than the rearview mirror in an automobile. The rearview mirror hopefully prevents that awful moment when the rider must turn his head backward to see what is happening behind him. That's a harrowing experience at best.

An accessory that has become a stock component for any motorcycle licensed for the street is the turn signal. It became mandatory for all street bikes beginning with the 1972 model year.

Most other accessories are either "dress up" items, kits for modifying the bike for specific use or comfort add-ons. Any dealer carries a full inventory of these products along with his supply of spare parts for repair or maintenance. For the do-it-yourself motorcycle owner, there are also speed shops and even motorcycle parts discount houses in nearly every major metropolitan area.

Adjusting the rear-view mirror, a very important safety device and one that is difficult to use properly on a motorcycle.

A WORD ABOUT MINIBIKES

What a great toy for a youngster! Right? It's small and doesn't travel very fast, so it must be safe. It's maneuverable enough to be operated in the driveway or even the front yard. Well, it's fun, all right, but a minibike can be one of the most dangerous toys a young boy can get from his doting parents.

It's one of the most ill-handling motorbikes there are. The average minibike has a wheelbase that is too short, wheels that are too small and a poor center of balance. Most minibikes are also top-heavy, giving them a natural tendency to want to crash. Even experienced riders have taken headers off them.

Some minibikes have a braking system that consists of a metal plate that rubs against the rear tire, which of course is made of rubber. Frames are often boxy and not intended for standing up to severe jolts. The standard power plant is a lawnmower motor,

Shoes are important in motorcycling, as shown here (left) where a well-protected foot, encased in a strong boot, is caught by a rock. Light foot-wear like tennis shoes (right) offers almost no protection and is not recommended.

which was never intended to be used in a minibike and consequently is subject to breakdown because of this harder use.

The manufacturers got together to define minibikes so that they could be differentiated from another popular class of recreation motorbike, the minicycle. They decided that a minibike generally has a tire height of 14 inches or less, solid disc hubs, a seat height of about 25 inches and a motor limited to about four horsepower. Some minibikes are very well constructed, but nearly all of them suffer from those handling deficiencies built into a short wheelbase, small wheel, top-heavy design.

At the same time, the manufacturers defined the somewhat safer and more reliable minicycle as a vehicle with a tire height of 18 to 23 inches, a two- or four-stroke motorcycle-type engine, spoked wheels that have standard motorcycle-type front and rear brakes, and a three-speed or slipped clutch transmission. Of course, there are smaller bikes that have one or more of the minicycle features.

As might be expected a minicycle costs substantially more than a minibike, but purchasers have often found that they have a safer product, less subject to failure and possible costing the same or less in the long run than a minibike.

BUYING A USED MOTORCYCLE

A good used motorcycle depreciates 10 to 20 percent the first year, but may not lose any value after that, which is a lot better than an automobile does. Still, there are good bargains to be found if the buyer is willing to take the time to search for what he wants, and if he is knowledgeable enough about mechanical things to know what problems to look for in a used motorcycle.

Our friend Bob Greene, editor of *Motorcycle Sport Quarterly*, once listed some handy guidelines to follow when checking out a piece of used machinery. Here is Greene's twelve-point recommendation on how to find serious trouble before buying it:

1   *Look for bearing failure, which shows up in the oil.*
    Take an oil sample out of the crankcase and pour it into a white porcelain pan and gently shake it around in the pan like a '49er looking for gold. If there are

Most motorcycle dealers also sell and license motorcycle trailers like this one.

metal particles in the oil, they will settle to the bottom, and you know that motor will soon be history.

2   *When firing up the motor, listen for strange noises.* If they are not readily apparent, take a screwdriver and use it as a stethoscope, placing the tip against the motor and putting your ear up to the handle.

3   *Pull on the drive chain.* If it can be taken off the rear sprocket, it's had it.

4   *Look for fork bearing wear.* Placing a block under the motorcycle, have someone sit on the saddle and shift his weight back and forth. Face the front wheel and grab the fork legs. Try to move them back and forth. They shouldn't move, unless the bike has had many miles or has been abused.

5   *Elevate the rear wheel and let it run free.* First, take each side of the tire and twist it back and forth. If there is real movement, there is wear in the swing arm pivot bearings. While you're in position, also spin the rear wheel and eyeball it, checking for a bent rim.

6   *Check frame alignment by sighting from the front wheel to the back with head down on the ground in front of the motorcycle.*

7 *Look for brake wear by checking the angle of the brake arm.* If it has a 90-degree angle or not much more, most of the adjustment is gone.

8 *Look undernearth the motorcycle for those invisible underside dents and flat spots.* They may not be important, but added to a lot of other problems they may.

9 *While underneath, look for telltale signs that the motorcycle has been repainted recently.* Sometimes that means it was painted to cover up crash damage. A new paint job could be an asset rather than a cover up, and it must be evaluated.

10 *Check the head cone bearing, which is between the top fork bracket and the frame.* While holding the brake on, rock back and forth. Touching the bearing with a finger, feel for any movement.

11 *Unbolt the zerk fitting and look at the grease.* If it is dry, chances are the bike was abused by its owner.

12 *Look at the battery case.* If there is a dirt build-up from the floor of the case to where it touches the bottom of the plates, the battery is probably not long for this world. Non-transparent cases can be judged by the condition of the fluid in the battery. Look out for muddy fluid. That's bad news.

So there we have it—how to buy a new or used motorcycle. It just takes common sense, a little advance planning, honesty and some healthy skepticism.

3

Learning to Ride Is Easy

The trouble with learning to ride a motorcycle is that most of us have to teach ourselves. Until recently there wasn't any organized movement like high school driver education for the novice motorcyclist. Today, fortunately, there are more than 2000 high schools in the United States offering some sort of motorcycle rider education. In the state of Minnesota attendance at a rider training school is mandatory. The U.S. Navy has recently adopted a program, and there are a number of universities which have a similar course of instruction.

All this is a drop in the bucket, however, when the number of students is compared to the number of new riders who enter the sport of motorcycling every year. Under the circumstances, it is amazing that the accident record hasn't multiplied itself out of sight. Claims of the National Safety Council to the contrary, motorcyclists have an excellent safety record, a record that has been achieved in the face of fantastic growth in the number of riders. Growth of motorcycling means only one thing—every new rider is somebody who hasn't ridden before. And the statistics tend to prove that new people are more likely to have serious accidents.

The reason rider education, or lack of it, seems to us to be neglected is based on our own experience. An importer lent us a 175cc bike for a weekend several years ago and, when we went to pick it up, asked almost as an afterthought:

A motorcycle salesman acquaints his young customer with the controls of a motorbike as he patiently instructs the beginning rider. Most new motorcyclists are taught to ride by members of their family, friends or motorcycle salesmen.

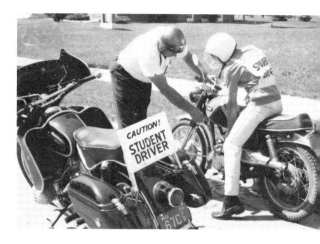

"By the way, have you ever ridden a motorcycle before?"

We had to confess, no.

"You won't have any trouble," the man said. "It's very simple."

Then he proceeded to give us the short course on the operation of a motorbike that was capable of speeds in excess of 70 mph. First he explained the controls, then asked us to ride in first gear around the parking lot next to his warehouse. He watched us make three perfect circles, and he congratulated us. He explained the operation of the gearshift and asked us if we wanted to try riding it around the block. Of course we did.

So off we went, riding this beautiful machine which had yet to record 10 miles on the odometer through one of the most heavily traveled industrial neighborhoods of Los Angeles during the afternoon rush hour. Not having had cause to think about the implications of what we were doing, we blithely rolled out into the maelstrom of tanker-trucks, homeward-bound passenger cars, buses and pickups. Meanwhile, we tried to practice smooth up- and downshifting and master the tricky feel of braking. Within five minutes we were smoothly moving along with the traffic at 50 mph.

When we returned to the warehouse, our smiling benefactor waved at us and said, "I think you've got it all right. Go on and ride it home. Remember, take it easy and you'll be all right."

Now the pressure was on. We suddenly realized that a couple of decades sitting behind the steering wheel of a wide variety of automobiles didn't mean anything anymore. We were going to have to travel from Point A to Point B, a distance of about 15 miles, on a motorcycle we barely knew how to ride. It meant concentrating on gears, throttle, brakes, traffic lights, other vehicles on the road, speed limits, pedestrians, small animals, wind resistance, changes in road surface from one block to the next, litter in the streets, potholes, side street traffic and all the rest. Meanwhile, we had to keep the brain racing to try to figure out the shortest, safest, least likely to be patrolled streets (we didn't want to attract a traffic ticket either) between the warehouse and home sweet home. That was the most careful and at the same time most exciting 15 miles we had ever covered.

Reflecting on the experience later, we guessed that this was equivalent to what many new motorcycle riders go through when they take their first ride. We wondered how many bad accidents are caused by sheer ignorance. Later, when we learned enough about motorcycles to realize what we had done while mingling with some of the most aggressive motor vehicle traffic in the world, the thought was frightening.

There are various gradations of motorcycle rider training. Most good dealerships train their salesmen to look for amateurs and give them rider familiarization courses whenever practical. The trouble is many "first time" customers have done just enough riding on borrowed bikes that they can't benefit from that minimum amount of instruction. One manufacturer, Yamaha, has organized familiarization riding into a regular school curriculum, with twelve hours of classes, mostly riding, spread over four consecutive Saturdays. Riders completing the course are also required to read a very good basic book, *Common Sense Tips for Safe Sportcycling*, by Jimmy Jingu and Don Gately. When they finish both, they are capable of passing any licensing test required in the United States. Many of the schools which have begun training programs, as well as the U.S. Navy, have adopted the Yamaha training format.

There is a school in Toronto that has far more stringent standards. Before graduation students must be able to handle obstacles, such as tire casings thrown in their way, and they are required to balance themselves on a teeter-totter while riding a motorcycle over it. The school emphasizes survival in a hostile environment, and in many ways that is what motorcycling is all about.

A father instructs his son and wife on the operation of a motorcycle.

In 1968 a branch of the Los Angeles City School System, the West Valley Occupational Training Center in Woodland Hills, California, became the first known public school enterprise to start a course in motorcycle riding. It is still in operation, the instruction consisting of six Saturday sessions for a total of twenty-four hours divided fifty-fifty between the classroom and the outdoor "laboratory." Cooperating with the center are the Motorcycle Industry Safety Council, the state's Motor Vehicle Department, the Automobile Club of Southern California, the Los Angeles Police Department and San Fernando Valley State College. If it weren't for the outside assistance, there would be no public school system involvement since the center is supposed to train men and women for employment. Graduates are advertised to the business community as safe, reliable messengers, but it is unlikely many of the students in motorcycle riding are taking the classes to prepare for a career as delivery boys.

All of these schools plus any others we don't know about couldn't handle more than 30,000 riders a year. In the state of California alone, from 1964 to 1969 motorcycle registrations increased 128 percent, from 208,362 to 476,919. And that doesn't even count off-road bikes that don't have to be registered!

So most of the new motorcycle riders are just going to have to do the best they can, seeking help from motorcycle salesmen, experienced riders, their local police traffic divisions and by reading various publications available on the subject.

Perhaps the first thing to learn about a motorcycle is that you shouldn't be in a big hurry to jump on it and ride it. Knowing the natural enthusiasm a person has for a new possession, that's easier to preach than to practice. We'll never forget that wonderful Christmas so many years ago when Santa Claus brought the first two-wheel bicycle to our house. We pushed it out to the sidewalk, finally taught ourselves how to flip a leg over it while it was rolling and started pedaling down the pavement. We were actually riding a two-wheeler! There was only one thing wrong—we neglected to learn what made it stop.

So when we got to the end of the block we did the only thing we could improvise on the spot. We aimed the bicycle for a bush and jumped off. After a few rides up and down the block, we got rather good at jumping off and crashing the bike on target—into a shrub. It was almost a letdown to learn that we were doing it wrong, that there was a brake to push on.

Fortunately, most beginning motorcycle riders do not practice

A woman runs through the operation of the motorcycle while it is still up on its kickstand, so that she will be thoroughly familiar with the controls when she begins to ride.

this sort of foolishness, but there are many examples of their making mistakes because of unfamiliarity with the machine, its controls, its handling characteristics and its safe operation. It is one thing to listen to a fellow say, "This is the brake, use it this way," and fully another to do it when you have to.

Instead of hopping on a motorcycle and learning the hard way, walk around it and look at it first, then climb on it, get the feel and try the controls.

The most important control is down at the right side on most motorcycles, below the footpeg. It is the foot-controlled brake for the rear wheel. The reason the rear brake is the most important one for a beginner to know is that operation of the front brake is a little tricky and needs getting used to. You should know enough about the front brake to stay away from it at first, if nothing else. It is operated by squeezing the lever on the outside of the right handlebar toward the handle bar.

Leaving the bike on its kickstand, hop on and sit in the saddle. Reach out and grip the handlebars while resting the feet on the footpegs. The right handlegrip is twisted to open and close the throttle. Outside the left handlegrip is the lever controlling the clutch. The foot opposite the brake manipulates the gearshift, which is usually three to five speeds forward. Not all gearshifts operate the same way. For specifics, consult the owner's manual. Most motorcycles have a kick starter on the right side, although some now carry an electrical starter.

Just as an automobile has an ignition key, so do most motorcycles. To start the bike after turning the key on, it is necessary to make sure the petcock found on the bottom of the fuel tank is turned to "on" so gasoline can get to the carburetor. Also make sure the transmission is in neutral. Some motorcycles have a green light on the face of the speedometer which turns on to indicate neutral. Otherwise, it's easy to tell by gently rocking back and forth to see if the rear wheel is free or locked. If it is free, you're in neutral.

If the motor is cold, be sure the choke is out all the way. Otherwise, it's a good thing to engage the choke at least part way when starting the bike. The choke should remain open only thirty to forty-five seconds, and the engine should be run a little above idle for two or three minutes until it warms up, sometimes longer for one of the bigger bikes. If the choke is opened too soon, the motor will probably die. If it is left closed too long, you'll soon know it, because the spark plug will foul.

All kick starters behave differently, and some work differently every time. For best results, crack the throttle about one-quarter of the way, then push down hard with the right foot. Leave the foot on the starter peg, because if it kicks back that will prevent a painful cut or bruise on the leg. The motor should start at least after the third kick. If it doesn't start, forget the whole thing. Something is wrong. Most smaller bikes, those up to 350cc, will be easy to start, and the kick starter is not likely to kick back. But if you're a conservative, you'll leave that foot planted on the starter peg to prevent kickbacks, just in case.

During the familiarization process, it is a good plan to have someone with you who knows about motorcycles, so you can ask questions, and so he can observe errors you make before it is time to try riding the motorcycle. When that time comes he should still be around because you never know when a helping hand might be needed.

A word of caution—the Yamaha Safe Rider Training Course, as well as many experienced teachers, specify a motorcycle no larger than 100cc for training the beginning rider. This may not be practical in individual cases, but it strongly recommended.

Having started the bike, it is time to disengage the clutch and shift into first gear by pressing the gear lever. The clutch should be released very slowly, while gradually increasing the throttle. It takes practice to do this smoothly, and the practice should be done on a wide open space, like a vacant parking lot or a large yard where there is nothing to run into. The trick is smoothness. Shifting is practically a lost art for automobile drivers in an age of automatic transmissions. The technique of shifting, mastered properly, can give you a fine sense of accomplishment.

Once in first gear the best exercise is to practice riding in a straight line at low speed for short distances, say 20 to 50 feet. Ride a short distance, pull on the clutch and use the foot brake to bring the bike to a full stop. It is difficult to balance yourself while going slowly, much more so at 5 to 10 mph than at 20 to

30. Don't be in a hurry to go fast. Slow first-gear riding is important to master. To make sure you are concentrating on a straight line and not wiggling all over the place, half out of control, practice riding toward your friend. The idea that he is keeping an eye on you will make you concentrate harder. He should remind you to keep your head up and eyes looking straight ahead, rather than down at the ground just ahead of the front wheel. Looking down is an easy habit to develop, and a bad one. Also, if he is directly in your path, his presence will make you practice using the brake. If you are going as slow as you are supposed to, there is no danger of hitting him, but in case of a problem, he should have plenty of room to back up and lots of space to move laterally, one way or another.

After coming to a stop, using the foot brake and disengaging the clutch, practice backshifting into neutral. Cultivate the habit of dropping into neutral every time you come to a full stop and putting a foot down.

The next exercise should also be done in first gear. With a friend standing in a stationary position make slow, even circles around him. This gives you a feel of the amount of lean it takes to turn a certain radius. After a few laps, turn and go in the other direction.

Now you're ready to work on shifting. Concentrating on the smooth application of both the clutch and the accelerator, ride in a straight line, shift up to second, brake, shift back down to first, then continue a short distance, brake and after a full stop shift into neutral. Stopping, shifting up and down and stopping again does wonders for developing co-ordination. Continue the shifting exercise up through the gears. The braking effect of engine compression will become quite apparent as you shift down, and you will learn how to slow the bike almost to a stop without using the brakes at all.

Merely knowing how to shift up and down and how to lean into a turn are not enough to familiarize the beginning rider with the potential usefulness of his machine. At this point it would be a good time to take a leaf from the Yamaha Basic Rider Training Course. At about the third lesson the instructor lines up a set of cones and has his students zigzag through them at low speed,

Right side lever (left) is the front brake, left side, the clutch.

left, right, left, right. Rocks or just about anything can be substituted for cones—tin cans, bricks, bottles. They should be placed fairly far apart at first, and after you find this easy to do, move them closer together.

Playing on an obstacle course which you can arrange any way it suits you, as long as it is level and has nothing solid to run into, has plenty of challenging situations and is not only fun but very instructional. While practicing on the course, be sure to have plenty of opportunities to practice braking. If you get tired of one layout, rearrange it. There is no such thing as too much practice.

When you feel confident enough during this period, gradually begin to use the front brake along with the rear brake, being careful to use them only when traveling in a straight line. Use them lightly at first until you get the feel of how the bike handles under front and rear braking.

After eight hours of this sort of riding, everything should feel more natural. You should have conquered the tendency toward jackrabbit starts, which are not only bad for equipment but potentially dangerous to the rider. You should understand about keeping the revs up in all gears to keep from lugging the engine. You should have practiced shifting into neutral every time you come to a full stop so that the procedure is automatic. You should be able to shift so smoothly up or down that the bike does not lurch. Now you're ready for the hardest part of all.

Cecil Zaun, a retired driving safety official for the Los Angeles City School System, once quoted a statistic we have never forgotten. He said that of 1500 motorcycle riders killed in 1967, 75 percent were riding rented or borrowed motorcycles. The implications are that (1) these riders didn't know their machines and (2) many really didn't know how to ride.

The point is this. All the familiarization in the world won't guarantee your safety out there where automobiles and trucks rule the streets and highways, and where a large number of drivers

Use of gearshift foot lever. Most motorcycles have a shifting system of pushing the lever down for shifting up and lifting the lever up with the toes for downshifting. Note the improper use of tennis shoes.

resent your taking up part of the space they feel entitled to. What you have equipped yourself with in this do-it-yourself motorcycle riding school is to handle the motorcycle smoothly and automatically. It's important that you do not have to stop and think every time you want to turn, shift or brake. It's important that you develop an ear for shift points so that you don't daydream down the street lugging the motor so badly that it won't respond when you suddenly wake up and need it to do something quickly.

Having become acquainted with the motorbike, you are aware without anyone lecturing you that it is uniquely safety-oriented in comparison with an automobile. A motorcycle takes up a tiny space and is very maneuverable, which can be a tremendous advantage in a tight situation. You have 360-degree visibility with no steel barriers in any direction. In traffic you sit higher than the man driving a car, and you can see what is going on farther ahead than he. You can accelerate better than anything on the road. If your bike is 250cc or less you can outbrake anything as well; big bikes have relatively the same stopping distance requirements as automobiles.

On the other hand, while riding a motorcycle you are barely, if at all, visible to the motorist, and everything you do on the street has to begin with the assumption he simply can't see you. Should you have a collision with a car, you are in deep trouble, because there is no doubt of the outcome of any scrap between a 4000-pound automobile and a 250-pound motorcycle. Your ability to stop quicker than a car puts you in double jeopardy, because you can avoid the sudden emergency situation up ahead oftentimes only at the risk of being run over from behind.

There is a third hazard in traffic, and it has to do with the incredibly bad driving habits of some motorists. While you are tooling down the street, trying to stay out of everybody's way, you never know when you are going to encounter a zombie at the wheel, a drunk or some psychologically disturbed individual who has it in for all motorcycle riders. We hate to mention this, but we reported a murder story for a newspaper once in which an enraged motorist actually chased a motorcycle rider with his gun blazing. He finally killed the bike rider.

So before rolling down the driveway into the street in front of the house to fetch a magazine at the drugstore, try to commit these universally accepted safety tips to memory.

1   *All the motor vehicle laws that apply to automobiles also are in force for motorcycles.* Drivers often take liberties with the law, but motorcyclists don't dare. Drivers coast through boulevard stops with their automatic transmission, but motorcycle riders have to stop, put their foot down and proceed. Any time a bike guy breaks, cracks or even bends a traffic ordinance, he runs the risk of alienating someone in a 4000-pound automobile.

2   *Assume you're the invisible man.* Nobody can see you at any time. It's not far from the truth. A motorcyclist makes a small image in the rearview mirror, or otherwise traffic officers wouldn't be able to sneak up on lawbreakers so easily. Once you take it for granted you can't be seen, then you begin to practice real, honest-to-goodness defensive riding. That's the right way.

3   *Pay attention to the surface on which you are riding.* Particularly keep an eye out for *changes* in the surface. The cyclist's biggest nemesis is the pothole. Where the pavement ends and the dirt detour begins, slow down and be careful or you'll be likely to spill. In many residential areas the cross streets bring with them gutters that crease the street you are riding on. In a car that gutter means a nasty bump, but on a motorcycle if you are not careful it means an airborne trip into a nearby tree. It is impossible to monitor the roadway if you are tailgating the car in front; so back off and give him room. Leave even more room if you are being tailgated because you are risking the chance that the fellow up front will slam on his brakes and turn you into a motorcycle sandwich.

4   *Railroad tracks need to be crossed perpendicularly, never at an angle.* Take it slowly as well. The same applies to streetcar tracks, where they exist.

5   *Avoid wet streets, rain, ice and snow.* If it's raining, park. Even motorcycle police don't go out in the rain on their bikes—they switch to patrol cars. In the event you approach a place where there is water in the street, slow down and proceed very carefully. If the water is deep, don't take chances; something might be hidden under the surface. Detour if at all possible. Water can be negotiated, but lots of skill is usually required. On country roads water and ice are often found on the inside of curves. The best way to handle them is to slow down and ride through patches of danger in a straight line. That means entering and leaving the turn as widely as safety permits and cutting to the inside.

6   *Look out for moving obstacles.* When George Tirebiter, the dog, chases a car, all he gets is the smell of the tires, but the part he likes best about the motorcycle is your leg. The temptation is to kick old George, but that just gives him a better shot at it and doesn't help you keep your balance. Well-practiced pooches even lead the motorcycle so that they can stay with it longer. The best thing is not to let them disturb you but to speed up and try to get out of range as quickly as possible. There is another type of moving hazard, the occasional child or pet who dashes out into the street in front of you. The only way to avoid this hazard is to plan ahead—keep an eye out for small people and animals as you ride down the street. Be particularly wary of ball games because the old rule still applies: A bouncing ball is always followed by a running boy. If the ball goes into the street, so will the boy.

7   *Beware of all cars making a turn, particularly a left turn.* This is a common cause of accidents, and a particularly tragic cause for the motorcyclist. The man turning left is trying to judge the oncoming traffic, and if he doesn't see the motorcyclist, he leaves that part out of his estimate. The best way to know when he is

A rider approaching a break in the pavement should look at this situation as if someone were waving a red flag. Motorcyclists should constantly evaluate the surface of the road ahead of them and be prepared for anything.

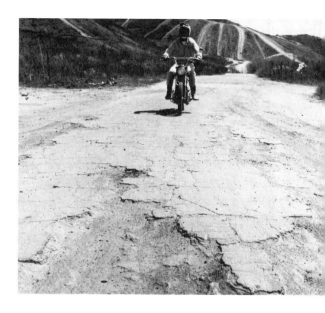

going to make a turn is to watch his face (is he looking at you, for example?) and his arms. The steering wheel can't move until they do. Meanwhile, slow down and prepare to use the brakes.

8   *Beware of all parked cars.* Imagine you're invisible to the man about to pull out into traffic. He's supposed to stick his head out the window and see if the way is clear, but nine times out of ten he won't. He may use his sideview mirror, but what if you don't show up in it? Keep an eye out for any car that has someone sitting in it. There is always the possibility someone will step out on the street side. A good number of motorcycle accidents involve the rider running into an opened car door.

9   *When riding in traffic, stay just to the left or right of the center of the lane.* The center is all slick with oil dropped by automobiles, but there are always two tracks where the wheels have picked up the oil and left a clean pathway.

10   *Driveways represent a special hazard.* Cars backing out of them usually can't see you and won't stop to let you by. Drivers turning into them seldom bother to use their turn signals—they're home, you see, and they have switched off their "obey the traffic laws" computer already. In a residential area, when following a car, give him plenty of room, and when he slows down, get ready. He may turn left or right into one of those driveways up ahead. You'll never know till he does it.

11   *Don't squeeze past cars in the "extra" lane that is wide enough for your bike but not for a car.* You take a chance on lighting that anti-motorcycle fuse for one thing. For another, you are a sitting duck for a lane-changer, a guy who accidentally moves over on you and catches a handlebar (that probably means good-bye), a fellow who forgot to signal he was going to make a turn at the next corner, or a traffic officer.

12   *Slow down at night.* Road conditions are even more

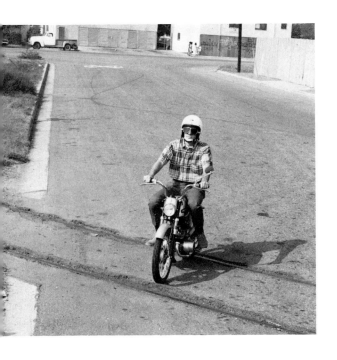

A smart rider demonstrates the safe way to cross railroad tracks (or any other irregularity in road surface) —perpendicular to the tracks, regardless of the direction of the road.

difficult to spot in the dark. The rule of thumb is never overdrive your headlight.

13 *Give a car plenty of room when passing him or when he is passing you.* The reasons are obvious. He can do a lot more damage than you can.

14 *Be prepared for anything.* Once some ghoul stretched piano wire neck high across a heavily-used motorcycle trail near Saugus, California. It was an almost invisible guillotine. Fortunately, the first rider who came along was alert. He thought he saw something and stopped. The wire hit him but only resulted in minor injury. Low branches can knock a rider clear off his bike the same way they did in old movies. Only when you do it instead of a Hollywood stuntman, it isn't funny.

15 *Be extremely careful about looking back.* Remember that at 40 mph if you look back for one second you will travel 59 feet before you face front again. Safety experts say it takes 44 feet at that speed to react to an emergency situation and another 88 feet to get stopped.

16 *Don't be distracted.* The advertising people who put up those billboards intended them for the fellow sitting in his air-conditioned sedan with power everything who is bored to death and welcomes a change of scenery every now and then. Even more tempting are the young, beautiful girls found strolling in every major city. We don't want to discourage birdwatching, but would recommend if there is something interesting enough to look at, stop and look, then proceed.

It is said that off-road riding is a lot safer because of the absence of cars, trucks, buses, children running into the street and many of the other hazards we have just listed, but safety is a relative thing. You're just as bad off lying in the weeds with a broken shoulder,

An off-road rider mounts his trail bike.

next to a mangled bike, 35 miles from the nearest house, as you would be if you were struck down at First and Main by a tank truck.

Let's go into some of the potential hazards of off-road riding.

1 *The very pleasure of off-road riding, aloneness in the wilderness, is also its main hazard.* Riding alone is asking for trouble. In fact desert races are set up so that patrols move in behind the competitors and literally "sweep" the landscape looking for fallen cyclists. An experienced desert rider will light a fire to signal his whereabouts. That can be a dangerous practice because of the hazard of brush and forest fires. So the best protection you can have is a buddy to ride along with you.

2 *Train yourself to expect the unexpected.* Even when traveling over familiar ground, be ready for anything. When you look out over a beautiful prairie it looks as smooth as glass, but when you ride over it you find

out differently. After a little experience you get to know that what will cause an accident the easiest is what you can't see. Rocks and low fences hide in the tall grass. Sheer dropoffs are just around the next corner. Hikers are a half-mile up the trail, and while they can hear you coming closer they might not know just when you are coming around the bend. Birds and insects can be expected to make random kamikaze dives at your face shield. Frightened animals may run into your path or in an extreme case launch an attack. Abandoned mine shafts and excavations are everywhere.

3   *Know where you are welcome and where you are not.* More and more open land is closing to motorcycle recreation. The reason is that bike riders before you have abused their welcome, and now farmers and householders take it out on you. They retaliate by calling the law and in some cases by taking the law into their own hands—with guns.

4   *Ride with knees hugging the fuel tank and feet on the pegs.* The temptation is to relax in the seat and let the knees hang out. The easiest way to fall off is to sit this way and let the feet dangle. It's a good way to break a leg as well. All good off-road riders lift their bottoms off the seat and come to a nearly standing up position. They can see better and they are ready for anything. They can get a better feel of what the bike is doing and can steer better. And they aren't risking compressed vertebrae every time the motorcycle bounces off a rock.

5   *Be careful with water.* Water hides things, just as grass does. If you fall off and lose consciousness in the dirt, you might be all right in a few minutes, but it would be tragic to do it in a brook and drown in six inches of water. When your bike goes down in the water, the abrupt temperature change could ruin your

engine, leaving you not only with a costly repair bill but stranded to boot. In shallow water the footing sometimes changes rapidly from a rock-lined bottom to soft mud or sand. Catch a front wheel in that and over you go, usually head first.

6 *Sand takes special technique.* You have to get moving fast enough not to bog down (the faster the bike travels, the higher it rides), but slow enough to keep on the lookout for hazards.

7 *Hillclimbing.* It's great fun to ride up a hill, because most off-road bikes can climb almost anything, with enough of a run at it. You lean forward, hit the throttle and soon you're up and over. There are two problems: stalling on the way up and what do you do when you get to the top. If something makes you stop on the way up, don't let the bike roll backwards under any circumstances. Drop it and get off. You might have to pick the machine up in pieces later but at least you'll be able to pick it up. There's another funny thing about hills. They always have another side, the one that goes down. If you hit the summit at 20 or 25 mph and there is a dropoff, what are you going to do? The best practice is to slow immediately at the crest to look the situation over for the downward run.

8 *Riding downhill.* Take it slow and easy, in a lower gear. Forget the front brake on a steep descent, unless you like to play leapfrog with 150 to 250 pounds of iron. Practice with shallow hills first to build up your confidence, then work your way up to the bigger ones. The most serious trouble you can have is an out-of-control ride down a steep, bumpy hill. There is no way to get off or away from the bike without serious injury. Just hang on and ride it out.

9 *Practice using the front brake at low speeds on level ground until you feel confident about handling the*

bike. Always remember the front brake works a lot better than the rear brake, a phenomenon that makes the wheels want to swap ends if braking isn't a smooth, co-ordinated motion. After a while, practice using them together until it comes naturally.

10   *On narrow, twisting trails keep the feet up on the pegs.* Never stick a foot out in a turn over rough terrain. It could catch hold of something and pull you right off the bike. What is caught could easily break.

11   *Learn to use the bike in every way—it can get you out of trouble.* That means learning to do "wheelies" and how to jump properly.

A rider cornering. Note the tennis shoes, which are not recommended, since they do not give adequate foot protection. (Courtesy, Yamaha)

A word about wheelstands or "wheelies": You may think of them as something to do to show off, but they have a definite function in off-road riding. The rider who knows how to ride balanced on his rear wheel can avoid many obstacles, such as rocks and fallen trees. With the front wheel in the air, all the shock is absorbed by the rear wheel and rear suspension. Directional stability is hardly affected at all.

The best place to practice wheelies is on an almost level but slightly uphill slope. While riding in first gear at low speed, stand up, lean forward and lift the handle bars firmly while giving a slight twist to the throttle. To prevent flipping over backwards, keep your foot on the brake pedal and be prepared to use it. Application of the rear brake brings the front wheel down. The most common mistake of new riders practicing wheelies is trying to do too much too soon. Don't try to see how high you can go. Just take things nice and easy. Otherwise you'll have a crippled piece of machinery and maybe a few injuries of your own to show for your efforts. Should the motorcycle loop on you, try to get off running so you won't be underneath when it comes down. When bailing out, be sure to let go of the handlebars and move laterally away from the bike.

Now about flying through the air: When approaching a jump you should be standing up on the footpegs, because you will need all the strength in your two legs to absorb the impact upon landing. Don't reduce power until you're in the air, then hit the throttle upon landing to keep the rear wheel from landing too hard. The most important thing is to keep the front wheel higher than the rear wheel, because if the front wheel lands first, you're in serious trouble. Although you cut the power while in the air, a blip of the throttle will assure you the engine is still working.

In all of the previous, concerning both street and off-road riding, it cannot be stressed enough that the machine should be kept in perfect running condition. Tires should be inflated to recommended pressures, fuel should be checked, the electrical system should be in good order and the engine properly serviced. It is also a good habit to go over the bike and tighten all the bolts every time you take it out. A little later in the book we will turn the subject of maintenance over to a real expert.

4

Survival Is No Laughing Matter

The average motorcyclist has a median age of twenty-two and rides 3000 to 5000 miles a year, mostly for recreation. He carries a passenger about one-fourth of the time, lets other members of his family use his bike 5 percent of the time and lends it to others to ride about 5 percent of his annual mileage.

The accident rate per unit distance traveled is slightly higher for a motorcycle than it is for a car, but the fatality rate is five times higher. Our average motorcyclist would be most likely to have his accident during the first six months he was riding. One-half of all motorcycle accidents involve riders with less than two years of experience.

In any motorcycle accident there is a high probability that a serious injury or fatality will result. The most common injury is to the head, which happens 150 percent more frequently than a leg injury and three times more often than an arm injury. The rider is almost always thrown off his bike in an accident. Those are the conclusions of a study conducted for the National Highway Safety Bureau by the Transportation Research Department of Airborne Instruments Laboratory in Deer Park, New York. There are probably later studies available, but this one covers the period of greatest growth in the use of motorcycles in the history of the United States, 1949 to 1966.

The most important fact brought out by the analysis is that

motorcycle riders have improved their record for traffic safety in the face of tremendous growth in the use of this type of vehicle.

In 1949 there were 31 million registered motor vehicles in the United States. By 1966 the population of automobiles, trucks and buses had more than tripled to 96 million. In the same period motorcycles increased in registration from 197,920 to an estimated 1.8 million or nine times as many.

Fatal motor accidents involving drivers, passengers or pedestrians increased 71 percent from 31,701 to 53,000, while during the same period motorcycle fatalities jumped 95 percent from 1,103 in 1949 to 2,160 in 1966.

Traffic fatality figures are tragic, of course, but the fatal motorcycle accident cloud has a silver lining. The research group at Airborne Instruments Laboratories found that fatalities per 10,000 motor vehicles on the road inched downward in that period from 7.09 in 1949 to 5.52 in 1966. At the same time the motorcycle fatality rate plummeted from a high of 23.03 to 11.28.

In other words, the risk a motorcyclist takes in getting hurt is still greater than the chances for a fellow who sits surrounded by all that steel in a sedan, but compared to the way things used to be when the risk was three times as great, definite progress has been made. One of the reasons for improvement of the record is that the everyday motorcyclist today is more likely to be a young, vital person with good reflexes, better than average eyesight and a healthy body that heals more easily.

The Airborne Instruments Laboratory study pointed out that 58 percent of motor vehicle drivers—and this group includes 90 percent of all persons in the United States over the age of sixteen —are male. By comparison, 93 percent of all motorcycle riders are male. According to the survey, the educational level of the motorcycle rider is higher, and since 35 percent of all motorcycle riders are under the age of twenty, the researchers concluded they had better eyesight and were in better overall physical condition.

A. D. Little, writing in "The State of the Art of Traffic Safety" for the Automobile Manufacturers Association, declared that driver error causes 80 to 90 percent of all motor vehicle accidents. In other words, nearly all traffic accidents can be prevented. For the sake of the motorcycle rider involved they must be prevented, because the odds of his coming out alive can be incredibly poor.

Once the relatively simple skill of riding is mastered, the rider must learn how to stay out of trouble. Operating a motorcycle has the effect of making a better citizen of the road out of a rider, because the motorcyclist is compelled to work harder at his practice of safety than anybody else.

It can be done. The California Highway Patrol reports that its motorcycle officers cover 8 million miles a year at the cost of 175 accidents. That amounts to one accident for every 45,000 miles under the most unfavorable conditions possible.

What are some of the serious problems that can confront a lone rider suddenly without warning? What should be done about them?

1   *Debris in the street.* Whenever traffic allows, the best thing to do is to stop and clean it off the roadway. If you run over something big or sharp enough, stop and check for tire or rim damage. Wire in the street can get wrapped into the spokes of a wheel or into the chain and cause a sudden stop. At the first suspicion of this, stop immediately and make an inspection. Check tires regularly for nails and broken glass.

2   *Objects that fall off cars.* If something looks loose and ready to fall, try to signal the driver about it. If he pays no attention, either stop and let him put some distance between you, or pass him and let the piece of his car drop where it won't do you any harm.

3   *Gravel, dirt and mud.* When such foreign matter projects out onto a highway from a construction site, for instance, it is a hazard that could cause your wheels to slide out from under you. Detour if you can or slow down and pick your way through. If it's really bad, stop.

4   *Median strips.* Stay away from both the concrete islands and the painted double lines, which are slick as glass. The same applies wherever a highway has an expansion joint in the center of the pavement.

5   *When you have to ride in the rain.* Wait fifteen or twenty minutes after it has started raining. This gives the rain time to clean oil and dirt off the surface of the pavement. If it is only drizzling, wait even longer.

6   *You are riding down the highway and suddenly a gust of wind hits you, knocking you off balance.* It wouldn't do that if you were paying attention to local weather conditions and the terrain. You can get socked with a gust of wind when you come out from behind a hill. Be braced for that. The effect can be just the same when you come out of the wind and go behind a hill. Compensating for a crosswind has made you lean into the breeze, and you have to stop leaning the instant you feel the wind stop.

7   A *dip in the road is ahead.* The one place you don't want to get airborne is on the highway. Slow down and take a good look at what's in the bottom from the entrance to the dip. It could be flooded, or there could be an accident or a stalled car blocking the road in there. You won't know until you look, and when you look you need to be going slow enough to stop if necessary.

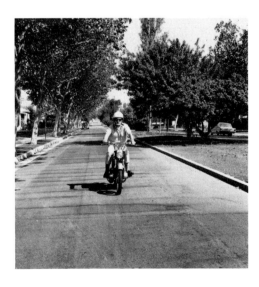

A street rider on a residential street.

8   *You are purring along a dirt road just below the foot-hills of a mountain range, and suddenly a washout looms ahead.* You are traveling too fast. The washout shouldn't surprise you, because you are paralleling the mountains, and you should not have to be told that every spring water runs down the mountains, not up.

9   *Approaching a signal.* Anticipate the amber (yellow) light. Don't try to speed up to beat the red unless the car behind you is tailgating and you have no choice. The one time you speed through the intersection, that will be the time Joe Dragster jumps the signal and collects you for a hood ornament.

10 *Sitting at the signal.* Don't leave the bike in gear. It should be in neutral. In first, with the clutch out, is the time the clutch cable might pick to break. The result could send you hurtling into the path of the cross traffic.

11 *Sitting at a boulevard stop with a car approaching from one side.* Wait long enough to see what he is going to do. He probably doesn't see you, and he may be in the habit of running that stop sign regularly. Let him go.

12 *You are truly the invisible man.* One way to improve the visibility situation is to use the headlight all the time, day or night. Some states require this. Many police departments burn headlights as a standard procedure. Even long haul buses do it.

13 *When taillights flash on ahead on the freeway.* Begin slowing immediately, before the chain of lights reaches the car in front of you. Keep tabs on the car behind you, which could scoop you up if conditions were right. Signal him by using the turn signals, left, right, left, right. Always look for someplace to get out of the way. That's why the fastest and slowest lanes are the best places to be. They offer convenient escape areas.

14 *A car decides to change lanes and occupy your space.* Back off or speed up, whichever is safest. But don't argue, move.

15 *In the country, a farmer pulls out of a side road directly into your path; there's no room to stop.* You have acceleration. If you see him coming, use it to get by him. If there is no traffic coming, use all the road you need to, but stay away from him. He's an accident looking for someplace to happen.

16 *You are starting to pass a car, and up ahead you see an obstruction blocking his lane.* Back off if you can. If you can't, move as far to the left as possible. Just figure automatically that he doesn't know you are there and will take evasive action—into your lane.

17 *You and your buddies are riding in the desert, very close together, when you go down in front of them.* Stay down and don't move until they get past or stop. At this point they can maneuver a lot quicker than you can. It would be a shame to get up and run into somebody's path after escaping injury in a fall.

18 *Cresting a hill.* Stay to the right. An automobile coming from the other direction will crowd the center line, anticipating a right or a left hand turn on the other side of the hill.

19 *Overtaking another motorcyclist.* Do it cautiously, giving him plenty of room. At highway speeds his rearview mirror may be vibrating so badly it is useless. He can't hear you because of the wind. If you come upon him too quickly, you will surprise him, and he may react by losing control. Sammy Tanner's rule of thumb is never pass anybody on the road more than 10 mph faster than he is going.

20 *When the throttle sticks.* Pull in the clutch lever, brake and kill the ignition. Get stopped. If the prob-

lem is dirt in the linkage, you can probably correct it. If not, park the bike until repairs can be made.

21 *Speed wobble.* There are many causes, but when the wobblies get you, the cause is academic. Accelerate quickly to get the weight off the front wheel. Hit the rear brake only, stop and get off. Check for a loose axle bolt, and check the steering dampener.

22 *Rounding a curve on a gravel road, you feel the rear wheel start to lose traction.* Turn the front wheel in the direction of the slide. That will keep the bike upright. Back off the throttle and dirt track it around. If you start to go down, don't hit the brakes. Put your foot out to slide on. Once the bike goes down, let go and push off. Get away from it.

23 *The sun is low, and alternate groves of trees cast dark shadows across the road between patches of bright light in the open spaces.* Visibility has deteriorated. Slow down. Your eyes are fighting it.

24 *The road is straight, the traffic is light and your mind is beginning to wander.* That is the first sign of road fatigue. You're lucky in a sense you are not in an old car that allows carbon monoxide to seep through the floor boards, making the driver even sleepier than you are. Avoid highway hypnosis by stopping about once an hour. Walk around, have a smoke or drink a cup of coffee. Break the monotony.

25 *A large bug chooses your face shield for a ticket to Heaven, splat!* Train yourself not to panic and not to take your hands off the handlebars. As soon as you can, stop and wipe the shield as clean as possible. Congratulate yourself for wearing eye protection. At the first sign of a rest room or water pump, stop and clean the shield thoroughly.

26 *You know you are going to crash into a wall or tree.* Lay the bike down. Locking the foot brake helps bring

various views of moto-cross racing

Leaping over an obstacle.

Stuck in the mud and out of the race.

The mass start at Hopetown, California.

Three riders duel through a turn.

Wrestling a moto-cross bike around a tight turn in the soft dirt.

the rear wheel around. Try to do it as soon as possible, because there is still a chance you will slide into the tree, along with the machine, if you are going fast enough when you land.

27 *You have crashed, and you took a sharp rap on the head.* Inspect the helmet for damage. If there is a scratch on the outside, there is a good chance of damage on the inside, where you can't see it. Do what the racers all do. Return it to the manufacturer for inspection.

There is no catalog of specific recommendations to cover every situation you will face. The foregoing are offered as guidelines, but what they amount to is common sense. In catastrophic situations, there is nothing to do but cast your lot with fate. Under identical circumstances one fellow will stand up, brush himself off and walk over to look at his crumpled machinery, while another will never move again.

The really serious rider will practice leaving his bike, laying it down at low speed to get the hang of it. A course in tumbling never did anyone any harm. Athletes who either have or who develop great co-ordination and dexterity have an advantage, particularly football players who are coached "how to fall." Why is it one fellow goes through life falling off ladders and walking under descending flower pots without suffering anything more than a bruise and a cut or two, while another poor soul finds a banana peel on the sidewalk and cracks his skull, or walks into a revolving door and fractures his leg once every six months? Call it chance or fate or luck. There may be more to it than that. We've seen the same youngsters hurt playing football too many times, while others who have taken harder knocks keep playing year after year with no time lost due to injuries.

How do you apply this to safety on motorcycles? First, you adopt a "stay out of trouble" attitude, avoiding situations you know you might have trouble handling. That means slowing down for corners and letting the pushy guy in the GTO cut in front of you on Woodward Avenue, and it means riding across the desert at moderate speed, expecting to find trouble and not making like

J. N. Roberts in the Mint 400. Second, you think about the tough problems you just barely avoided and try to analyze what you would have done if . . . Third, you practice simple things like laying the bike down, taking pains to do it at slow speed on a soft surface so you won't hurt your equipment or yourself. The experienced racer, by the way, leaves his bike with his head down, protected by his shoulders. Fourth, you try to work yourself into the best physical shape possible.

Did you ever look closely at professional motorcycle riders? There is hardly a pound of blubber among one hundred of them. The best pros are lean and muscular. They have to be to maintain the stamina and take the body punishment that racing demands. Ask any rider, and he'll probably tell you he doesn't work out at a gym or play handball or jog. He just rides a lot, and that keeps him in shape. One thing is certain, he didn't start racing motorcycles out of condition.

The Airborne Instruments Laboratory safety study declared that the average rider puts 3000 to 5000 miles of wear on his bike every year, compared with 9000 to 12,000 for the average automobile driver. But what the safety researchers didn't break down was the mileage each person drove or rode purely for pleasure

Lace-up shoes or boots are the most highly recommended footwear for motorcycle riders. Lace-up boots are preferable to pull-over boots because in the event of an injury they can be removed more painlessly.

and the mileage covered because he had to. We suspect the ratio would have been reversed, with maybe 2000 miles of motorcycle riding for fun every year and less than half of that for automobile recreation.

What this implies when placed next to the accident statistics is that the motorcycle jockey is out having fun and hurting himself more often than the motorist, who is mostly driving back and forth to work or school. That's an exaggeration, but it means something to a cautious rider who is interested in keeping his head intact and his bones in one piece. It means you don't take your mind off what you are doing while riding a motorcycle for one second. It means you don't take your mind off what all the other people are doing around you, not for one second. It means more than defensive driving. It means, "Think survival."

A WORD ABOUT PROTECTIVE CLOTHING

We mentioned earlier the importance of the safety helmet, proper footwear and gloves. The helmet is an essential, because it can mean the difference between life and death in even the simplest of accidents. We knew of a beautiful young lady who was a national kart racing champion as a teenager. She won two hundred trophies in the course of a few years, traveling around the country with her father and brother. At the age of eighteen and recently married, she won a race that had as first prize a smallbore motorcycle. On her first time aboard, one-half block from her home, she was riding the new machine at 5 mph when she had an accident, hit her head against a utility pole and was killed.

This young woman was not unfamiliar with crash helmets. She had worn one from the time she was thirteen years old, but for some reason she failed to wear one that fateful day. Here was virtually a professional racer, who had thousands of miles of competition behind her, but she was careless. Her father claimed her life would have been saved by the helmet she left at home.

A salesman we know sold a bike to a fellow who was short of cash. He tried but couldn't sell the customer a helmet. Two months later the customer came in and bought the helmet. On the way home a car turned in front of him, and the rider went sailing headfirst over the hood. He stood up, dusted himself off and rode back to the dealership.

"I just wanted to say thanks," he said to the salesman.

It has taken a while for the word to get around about foot protection, as well as helmets. Our library includes safety books and pamphlets that show riders without head protection and wearing a variety of footwear from sandals and high heels to loafers, ballet slippers and tennis shoes. The most startling photograph of all shows a father on a minibike giving a ride to his son, who is balancing sidesaddle on the fuel tank in front of pop, and his daughter, who is riding on his shoulders. There isn't a helmet in the bunch.

For street riding, ordinary leather shoes are acceptable, but lace-up boots are recommended. A compromise is the pull-over boot, the zip-up boot or high-top shoe, because they give ankle protection. Off the road, nothing but a lace-up boot is recommended.

The ideal body protection, of course, is the leather suit, which costs anywhere from $50 to $150. Keeping in mind that after a head injury the most likely part of the body to need protection is the leg followed by the arm, a set of leathers is a good investment. In lieu of leathers, the next best protection is full-body coverage, that is, long pants and a long-sleeved shirt, preferably covered by a jacket, sweater or other outer garment. T-shirts, short pants, miniskirts, bathing suits and hot pants are stylish, but they beg for trouble on a motorcycle.

A lady who really went looking for trouble was the attractive young woman who was first seen in the vicinity of York Boulevard and San Pasqual Street in the Highland Park district of Los Angeles early in the morning on April 30, 1952, wearing nothing but goose pimples. The Los Angeles Police Department unit which first spotted her was eagerly joined in pursuit of the carefree cyclist by other police from Pasadena and South Pasadena. She lost them a couple of miles away after a chase that was described on the police blotter as "enthusiastic."

The problem with lecturing about the proper clothing is that the manufacturers' advertising doesn't always agree with what they preach in their safety literature. In a typical month's issue of a popular motorcycle magazine we found ads showing a blond wearing knee high pull-over boots and hot pants, a brunette in white boots, hose and a two-piece sports outfit that exposed most of her legs, a woman in a miniskirt and a hatless young man on a bike displaying his colorful and proper street jacket. That's Madison Avenue for you.

CARRYING PASSENGERS

See the nice daddy.
He rides a motorcycle.
Ride, daddy, ride.
Look at Johnny.
Johnny is with daddy.
He holds onto daddy.
Smart Johnny.
Daddy is smart too.
He wears a helmet.
If daddy falls off, he won't hurt his head.
What if Johnny falls off?
Johnny has no helmet.
Daddy is not so smart after all.

How many times do we see the young motorcyclist riding down the boulevard, fully covered from helmet to proper boots, with his scantily clad girlfriend clinging to him? Some smart guy. He is just as bad as the father who gives the kid a ride on the motorbike without equipping him with at least as much protection has he knows he must have.

Passengers need the same protection against injury that the rider does, and they need a few words of caution as well. Riding double is a whole new game. Let's think about it for a minute.

1   *The handling geometry is drastically altered by a passenger.* Take a 250-pound motorcycle, add a 150-pound male, and the total is 400 pounds, but add a 110-pound female and suddenly it's up to 510. That's asking a lot, even of a finely crafted piece of machinery.

The weight, however, is not nearly so critical as where you put it. It has to go over the rear wheel, because that is where the extra sitting room is. Suddenly there is more strain on the rear shocks, more weight up high altering the center of gravity, more load for the tires, wheels and spokes, more pull for the engine and less efficient steering because the front end is lighter.

2 *Braking efficiency is lowered.* More weight means more inertia. Not only is the rolling mass more difficult to stop, but any sudden need to stop means the motorcycle stops quicker than the two people it is carrying. Your passenger will be pushing forward against you in an emergency with possibly disastrous results.

3 *Turning can be an adventure.* Unless the passenger is practiced enough to let you do the leaning and not fight against you or try to help and thereby lean too much, you will find cornering much more unstable. Tell the passenger to let you do the work and just go along for the ride. The best place for him/her to lean is onto you.

4 *Where do the extra feet go?* Not all bikes have an extra set of footpegs. To carry a passenger, make sure yours does. Tell the person in the back seat to keep their feet up on the pegs when you come to a stop and put your foot down. It's difficult enough balancing the extra poundage without having to fight a wiggle worm. As for youngsters, the very young can't reach adult footpegs. Build on a set just right for those little ones who ride with you. It's not hard to do.

5 *Panic.* "Ho, ho, ho! I'm sure scaring her." Those could be nice words for an epitaph. The frightened passenger wants off, now, and might do just anything. You could both go down, or he/she could "step off" at 40 or 50 mph with predictably terrible consequences.

6 *Steep climbs*. Don't try them. You're asking for a fatal accident. We've already lived through that mistake, thankfully. The weight is too far back on the rear wheel for the bike to get proper traction up a steep hill. Leaning forward helps, but usually not enough.

7 *Holding on*. One answer is to install a buddy bar, but the best method is a locked hand grip around the middle, as long as it isn't a death grip that squeezes the wind out of the operator.

There is nothing amusing about a motorcycle accident, particularly one with more than one rider on a single bike. Riding double is no time to do tricks, race or clown, because the punch line to the joke could be grim.

In 1952 the Road Research Laboratory of Great Britain worked out a scale of danger for the known forms of transportation. Motorcycles topped the "risk of death" scale at a magnitude of 40. Next came bicycles at 14, airplanes at 7, automobiles at 1, trains at 0.2 and passenger ships at a fraction so small it was called "negligible."

Riding double can be enjoyable, but safety is important. Note that both the operator and passenger are wearing head, eye, arm and leg protection. The girl is holding the operator around the middle, which is the safest way to hold on. Riding double is not for beginners. It requires special precautions and the use of common sense.

5
Simple Owner Maintenance

In 1962 Bill Krause was an auto racing driver with a great future. He had won the prestigious Los Angeles Times Grand Prix at Riverside, California. He had been Carroll Shelby's first test driver for the Cobra, and he had been one of General Motors' first test drivers for the Corvette Sting Ray. He had gone to the Indianapolis Speedway to drive in the "500" for Mickey Thompson and had been offered a chance to race a Formula 1 car in Europe.

With a small nest egg he had put away from his race winnings and income he had earned working long, hard hours, Krause bought a franchise to sell Honda motorcycles, and he turned his back on what was considered at the time to be one of the most promising careers in motor racing. Starting in a 1400-square-foot building with one employee, he built one of the nation's most successful motorcycle dealerships. The motorcycle business was as fast-growing then as it is today, but very few people could have predicted then the tremendous potential of the sport of motorcycling—a potential on which Bill Krause and others in the industry have built their fortunes.

Today Bill Krause has forty-nine employees in a complex that covers 20,000 square feet—almost half a city block—in Inglewood, California. Bill Krause Enterprises, Inc., the parent company, manufactures and markets motorcycle accessories and operates Bill Krause Sportcycles, a dealership which sells Honda, Triumph and Yamaha motorcycles. The Krause service department has been called by many in the industry the finest retail service facility in America, and it is certainly at least one of the best. It is a showplace. Because of his reputation for good service and his experience as an instructor and a lecturer, we called on Bill Krause of Bill Krause Sportcycles, Inglewood, California, to contribute this chapter on owner-maintenance of the motorcycle.

BILL KRAUSE

Rider maintenance can save many expensive trips to the local dealer for major repairs. Quite often these repairs would not have been necessary if the proper owner service had been performed.

Before we discuss the details of rider service, I think it would be in keeping to give a brief description of the differences between motorcycles or sportcycles and the more familiar automobile. The first and most obvious differences are the size and the lack of two wheels which render the bike unable to stand by itself without some sort of prop. While these are easy to recognize, there are many less noticeable to the inexperienced layman. Some of the more pertinent yet often overlooked characteristics are related to the comparatively small displacement of the engine. Also motor-cycle engines, with few exceptions, are air-cooled. Most beginners start on small one- or two-cylinder models ranging from 60 to 125cc which after a few weeks of getting used to are usually run at maximum speed and throttle opening. The latter may cause a relatively new rider some exciting problems when riding a friend's larger cycle for the first time. Due to these conditions, and the small amount of lubricant carried, it is imperative to maintain proper oil levels and use the best lubricants available.

Items requiring frequent checking are the control cables, rear chain and oil level. Motorcycle engines vary with regard to the number of cylinders including the now famous three-cylinder models which seemed impossible to build only a few short years ago. There are, however, really two basic types, the more traditional 4-cycle model and the now equally popular 2-cycle models. In order to understand the differences in these engines, it is important not to confuse the word cycle with the word cylinder as they are totally separate entities.

First let us briefly explore the 2-cycle engine. While 2-cycle engines may vary as to cylinder arrangements, the principles remain basically the same. The 2-cycle engine fires each time the piston reaches the top of the stroke or, more accurately, a few degrees before top dead center. The principle does not allow time for valves as used in 4-cycle engines to operate before the next power stroke. This enables the 2-cycle engine to have a simple cylinder head design which is really just a cap for the cylinder containing the spark plug and providing a combustion chamber with external cooling fins. As you can see, this type of engine has no conventional valves to adjust, and therefore, it is a simple design requiring few adjustments.

Most 2-cycle engines used in motorcycles are of the piston port type, which means the piston actually performs the job of any other piston and also acts as the valve controlling the air-fuel mixture both on intake and exhaust. Some manufacturers prefer to use the rotary valve system on most of their 2-cycle engines while others such as Yamaha only use this principle on engines of small displacement. A rotary valve is usually a rotating flat disc with sections removed to allow the air-fuel mixture to enter at specific times, thus providing a more positive control. While this is an advantage from a technical point of view it also requires some maintenance and often leads to the carburetor being mounted on the side of the crankcase. This can be somewhat clumsy in appearance and the extra width may interfere with trail riding.

The one thing all 2-cycle engines have in common is the lack of lubricant stored in the crankcase, as the incoming air-fuel mixture must pass through here prior to being transferred into the cylinders. This in turn means the engine must get its lubricant with the fuel by the pre-mix method or through a total loss oil system. These systems meter to the engine minute, but adequate, oil which is consumed along with the fuel. One of the most common problems with new or very old 2-cycle engines is that the oil supply exceeds the ratio tolerable by the spark plug causing a fouled plug condition. This can usually be remedied by using a spark plug having a hotter heat range than would normally be recommended, or by reducing the normal lubricant. Be sure to solicit expert advice before attempting to make such a change, as serious engine damage may result if proper precautions are not taken.

As we have previously mentioned, due to the design characteristics of the 2-cycle engine, oil or lubricant is passed through the engine and out the exhaust pipe or muffler. These engines therefore require periodic cleaning of the exhaust system. Most current 2-cycle motorcycles used for street or a combination of street and off-road use have an oil injection system which automatically meters oil into the engine. In this case the basic responsibilities of the owner are using the correct type of lubricants and diligent checking of the oil reservoir.

A critical thing on 2-cycle engines is to maintain the proper ignition timing and point gap. This will minimize the possibility

Most motorcycles come equipped with a small tool kit. Be careful when using other tools, since American wrenches, based on inches, often do not fit foreign nuts based on the decimal system.

Rear drive chain should be inspected regularly according to instructions in the owner's manual.

Chain is tightened by loosening the axle nut and then using adjuster screws at the rear of the swing arms.

of excessive heating and help assure maximum performance. While timing is a relatively simple thing, it must be done with good equipment and careful attention. This adjustment should normally be performed only by an expert or after counseling by a professional. While there may be many variations in these engines the basic principles as explained here are the common denominators. The generally accepted rule of thumb is that 2-cycles lend themselves better to off-road use while the conventional 4-cycle is more widely accepted for touring.

Tire pressures should be checked regularly. A pressure gauge is recommended, as service station gauges are frequently inaccurate.

While 4-cycle engines as applied to motorcycles are much the same as those used in the automobile, they must perform at greater efficiency per cubic inch.

The Japanese have pioneered production of overhead cam engines of small to medium sizes which are designed to operate at very high rpm. These engines produce unusually high horsepower relative to their size. Other than the various cylinder arrangements these engines also vary in the placement of the camshaft, which is the heart of the valve mechanism. Motorcycle camshafts, as in automobiles, are often re-worked by hop-up enthusiasts seeking more power. There are two basic locations for the camshaft, either in the crankcase using cam followers and pushrods to reach the valves or in the cylinder head itself. As we previously mentioned, all modern Japanese 4-cycle engines have them located in the cylinder head, while most English cycles use the pushrod system. The most popular arrangement, used in Japanese cycles, consists of a single camshaft with a rocker arm for each valve. These rocker arms have an adjusting screw for setting valve clearances, which needs periodic checking.

Now that you have a basic understanding of the two types of powerplants used in modern motorcycles, you will find that the controls and chassis of most cycles are basically the same.

If you happen to be the proud owner of your first motorcycle, it is important to study the owners manual before attempting any adjustments. Whether you have a new or used cycle, one of the best ways to detect problems before they become serious is to keep it clean. Keeping your bike clean will naturally enhance its value and encourage your pride of ownership as well. Because of the many exposed parts on a motorcycle, it is more complicated to clean and more vulnerable to damage as a result of carelessness. It is best to use a soft rag to remove mild road dirt and normal contamination. If excess dirt or mud has collected, it will require

Spokes also need constant attention. Bill Krause recommends checking the spokes by spinning the wheel free and listening for a ring. If only a few are loose, they can be tightened by a "non-expert," but if most or all of them are loose, it is wise to have a pro do the job.

washing with water and a mild detergent. Extra caution must be used when rinsing your bike to prevent damage to air filters and contamination of oil reservoirs and carburetors. Many cycles have been damaged extensively by well-meaning but uninformed sons or daughters who cleaned Dad's bike. One such example might be filling the exhaust pipe and subsequently the engine with water. After washing with water be sure to dry the exterior and run the engine as soon as possible, both to prevent moisture from entering the engine and to circulate the lubricants. The painted and chrome parts should never be cleaned with an abrasive; a good paste wax offers the best general protection for these items. Many of the aluminum cases are coated with a clear lacquer. Care should be taken not to remove this, as it will result in oxidizing of the exposed surfaces.

With few exceptions, sportcycles are equipped at the factory with small but adequate tool boxes and tool kits. These tools are designed to encourage owner maintenance and allow emergency repairs to be handled by the rider. Since most motorcycles sold in the United States are imported, it is seldom that American wrenches will do a proper job. There are three basic bolt size designations used throughout the world, the American fractional sizes, the English Whitworth sizes and the metric system. The metric system is currently in use by most countries with the exception of British Territories and the United States. It is important not to try to mix any combination of these, even though a few can be interchanged, as permanent thread damage may result. Remember the old adage, "Don't put a square peg in a round hole."

Providing you now have a brief understanding of owner maintenance, here are a few of the operations that can be performed using the tools supplied with the cycle.

It would first be wise to check your owners manual to see if it is the correct one for your cycle. If you find you do not have the correct manual, it would be well worth your effort to obtain one from your local dealer or distributor. The owners manual usually has a page or two describing the tools supplied with the cycle for your comparison.

Before you start off on your cycle you should always check all

Rider adjusts brakes, spark plug,

handle bars and front shock absorbers.

Checking and adjusting bolts and other parts of the motorcycles should become a routine for the bike owner.

cables and controls for proper adjustment. Most cable adjustments can be easily made at the control by turning the cable housing receptacle in or out for proper free-play.

Rear drive chain adjustment is normally controlled by the position of the rear axle. It is necessary to loosen the axle nut or nuts before attempting to tighten the chain by using the adjuster screws at the rear of the swing arms. After making the adjustment to the chain be sure to check the rear brake free play as this will be affected by moving the wheel. Installation of an oversize rear tire may require additional chain links or a half link to provide adequate tire clearance. This brings to mind the importance of maintaining the recommended tire pressures which are of extreme importance on a motorcycle. The handling, safety and tire life are directly related to tire pressure and terrain. Another important item related to tires and safety is the tightness of the spokes. This can easily be checked by spinning the wheel while holding a metal object against the spokes. Spokes having the proper adjustment should have a slight "ring" as they make contact with the metal. If only a few spokes are loose, they may be tightened to achieve the same tone as the others. If all or most of the spokes are loose, the wheel should be removed and re-trued by a professional.

In order to have the reliability we all expect from our cycles, there are certain things we take for granted on our automobiles which require watching on a motorcycle. Because of the greater heat generated in the cylinder heads of air-cooled engines, and

Careful attention must be paid to motorcycle tires. A rider inspects the valve to find stem damage (left) which is terminal. He looks at the tire casing to check for damage after a particularly bad jolt (right).

other related factors, spark plug life is greatly reduced. The average life for plugs on most touring bikes is from 1500 to 3000 miles. When checking the plugs, it is also possible to determine whether the engine is running too rich or too lean. Excess oil deposits may reveal such things as bad piston rings. Spark plugs which have a light gray or white color around the center electrode would indicate a lean condition. A black smudgy look would normally be due to an overrich condition which may be caused by a wet or dirty air filter. For air cleaner maintenance it will be necessary to refer to the owners manual as there are too many different types to go into here.

Because of the limited space and weight factors on motorcycles, batteries have limited storage for electrolyte and require frequent attention to liquid level. Most Japanese batteries have a clear plastic case with fluid level lines for easy checking, and they are usually located under the seat.

A simple thing like dirty ignition points will cause an otherwise perfect cycle to become inoperable. If you are not experienced enough to set the point clearance, it is a simple job to clean them with contact cleaner and get your cycle running.

One of the best investments you can make, if you intend to do your own maintenance, is an impact screwdriver. This is necessary to remove the cross head screws which are installed at the factory with power tools. The heads of these screws are usually ruined when trying to remove them for the first time with an ordinary screwdriver.

If you are an off-road rider only, the information contained herein would also apply to you. However, special attention should be given to items such as air cleaners, fork seals, spokes and chains. Riding in the high desert or mountains may require changing to a smaller main jet for peak performance. A word of caution, however, don't forget to change back to normal jetting when returning to lower elevations. Please remember that a louder motorcycle is not necessarily a faster motorcycle. When in doubt, always refer to your owners manual instead of asking your buddy. With a little owner maintenance, your cycle should give many miles of trouble-free riding with only occasional visits to the professional bike doctor.

6
Safety. Ecology. Law. and the Cyclist

The consumer revolution in America began innocently enough with the quiet settlement of a lawsuit by General Motors Corporation over the issue of whether the Corvair was or was not inherently a safe automobile. Word of the out-of-court settlement leaked out. Bill Huddy, news director of television station KEYT in Santa Barbara, California, where the plaintiff lived, revealed it to the world one night.

Lawsuits of that type are usually settled with the understanding that the person who filed the action will take the money and keep his mouth shut. The winners often sign a legal document agreeing to keep quiet or give back the money. For some reason, this procedure wasn't followed.

Soon came Ralph Nader and his book, *Unsafe at Any Speed*. The automobile, symbol of American affluence, started coming under critical examination. Accident statistics suddenly assumed political importance. Junk yards filled with car bodies became eyesores to the public which had once ignored them. Air pollution acquired new importance as a menace to public health. Some politicians attacked the internal combustion engine as one of the chief sources of peril in modern society. It is important to know the background that led to a new attitude toward "protective" legislation in order to understand governmental scrutiny of the role of the motorcycle today.

Even in a free society we all welcome some government control. Without it there would be chaos. Imagine riding down a street on either side, with no stop signals at the cross streets, oncoming traffic weaving its way toward you, no hand or blinker signals to warn you of sudden moves by the other fellow and no policeman to take charge in the event of an accident. That would be totally disastrous.

By and large motorcyclists have accepted traffic regulations as a necessary part of the scheme of things. What alarms many of them is the sudden attention lawmakers are paying to other aspects of the sport of motorcycling. Let's look at the legal side of motorcycling, especially the more modern trends:

SAFETY

Traffic enforcement and accident investigation officials have been viewing the motorcycle situation with alarm for years, particularly since the postwar boom has introduced so many new riders into street traffic. Work toward defining the problems and seeking solutions has intensified under the National Highway Traffic Safety Administration of the U.S. Department of Transportation. Riders can take some solace in the fact that the NHTSA's chief executive, Douglas Toms, is a motorcycle enthusiast himself.

Gradually, however, a pattern is emerging that indicates the motorcycle rider of the future will have to put up with more and more control. The federal government and many states are trying to set up uniform licensing standards and to start some kind of systematic training. So far, the state of Minnesota has the only worthwhile educational program, but it is only about as thorough as the usual high school driver education course. The student is taught how to ride safely, but he isn't instructed as thoroughly as he might be about the possibly catastrophic situations he may face later on. Whatever training program is finally agreed upon by all fifty states, nobody quarrels with the idea of having one.

There is, however, controversy over so-called compulsory helmet laws. So far, only seven states (California, Illinois, Iowa, Mississippi, Montana, Nevada and Wyoming) have no law at all. While New Mexico requires helmets on all passengers and all riders under eighteen years of age, Kansas' law applies only to operators and passengers over twenty-one, and Utah applies its regulation only to those public roads where speeds exceed 35 mph. The Utah statute was tested in its State Supreme Court, which found that injuries to a motorcyclist are a matter of public concern.

Justice A. H. Ellett wrote in part in his majority opinion: "Both hospitals and relief rolls are crowded. Any measure which would protect the operator of a motorcycle would tend to avoid collisions with other traffic on the highway."

He somewhat confused a safety device intended to work during a collision with the actual avoidance of that collision, but he touched upon a tender subject with the taxpaying public—that the lone motorcyclist does more than endanger himself when he goes without head protection. He risks the expenditure of public funds to care for him in the event of an accident. In that way he theoretically represents a menace to society unless he is made to conform.

Justice J. Allan Crocket dissented, writing: "If the conclusion is based upon the possibility that cyclists may become hospitalized, or on welfare, that opens a wide door indeed to paternalistic controls over innumerable aspects of human conduct as to what may or may not be good for one's individual health, morals or safety."

The safety helmet manufacturers also are not all four-square for

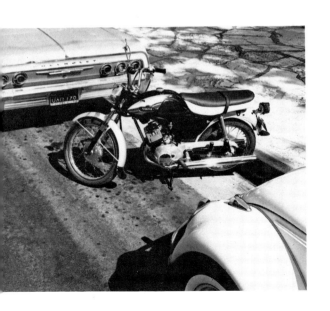

This fellow is asking for trouble. He parked his motorcycle in a space too small for a car, but he is close enough to take a hit from the Chevy in front or the VW behind—or both when they pull out.

mandatory helmet laws, believe it or not. One prominent manufacturer offered the opinion that mandatory laws would be bad for the industry, because they tend to encourage the starting of fly-by-night companies which jump in when the demand is high, market inferior products and then drop out when demand falls, leaving the good companies weakened. Meanwhile, thousands of motorcycle riders would (under this line of reasoning) be wearing helmets which do not meet rigid safety standards, and they would have a false sense of security.

The motorcycle industry lobby in California pulled off an interesting stunt to make its point about the mandatory helmet law. State legislators were all issued safety helmets and asked to wear them for a day. The uncomfortable representatives of the people quickly disposed of the bill by burying it in a committee. There are an estimated 1.5 million motorcycles registered and unregistered (off-road) in the state. That amounts to something between 20 to 25 percent of all the motorcycles in this country. A California helmet law would have had a profound effect on both helmet and motorcycle industries.

The fact remains that with forty-three of the fifty states requiring helmets and an increasingly protective attitude by government officials, it may be only a question of time before helmets are strapped on to avoid traffic citations everywhere in the United States.

Twenty-eight states currently have laws requiring eye protection for the motorcyclist, although two of them—Michigan and Washington—only require goggles or face masks at speeds above 35 mph, and Utah's statute applies at any speed on a road with a speed limit over 35. Those states which have no law requiring eye protection are Alabama, California, Idaho, Indiana, Iowa, Kansas, Maine, Massachusetts, Minnesota, Mississippi, Missouri, Montana, Nebraska, Nevada, North Carolina, North Dakota, Oregon, South Dakota, Texas and Wyoming.

Licensing remains the biggest single factor in efforts to improve motorcycle safety. Few states have a stiff examination, and only thirty-six have any special license or testing procedure for motorcycle operators at all. We went to a California Department of Motor Vehicles office to get a book and bone up for the motorcycle exam one day. The licensing examiner had to apologize and state that he had never seen one. We called another office, and the woman who answered the phone said that of course there was such a book, but she had been out of them for several months. They were on order and were expected any day now.

Despite the fact that many states have been lax in the licensing department, it is only a matter of time before there will be some form of licensing everywhere in the U.S. Just as the licensing requirements for automobile drivers have varied all these years, there will probably never be standardization unless the federal government steps in. And don't think that might not happen!

Not all states have laws affecting passengers on a motorcycle, rearview mirrors and other safety-oriented regulations. Twenty-nine states have some form of safety inspection, either at the time the motorcycle is licensed or more frequently. Some states either have laws or interpretations of other safety regulations that inhibit the builders of so-called "choppers," the homemade hot rods of two-wheeling.

NOISE

At the time this is written there are twenty-two separate motorcycle noise abatement bills in the legislative hopper in California, where much of the pioneering is done as far as motor vehicle law is concerned. As a practical matter, only one or two of them have a chance to be enacted, but the number of proposed statutes—and the number of different lawmakers who have proposed them—is a good indication of the mood of the public on the subject of excessively noisy motorcycles.

In California, where the standards are at least as strict as they are anywhere else currently, Section 23130 of the Motor Vehicle Code allows a maximum of 82 decibels for a machine traveling 35 mph or less, and a maximum of 86 for a bike more than 35 mph unless it is defined as a "motor driven cycle." Decibel levels for that type of bike are restricted to 76 dbA at 35 mph or less, and 82 dbA above 35.

Russ Sanford, the motorcycle enthusiast's only paid lobbyist, reports that the trend in new legislation is to reduce decibel levels. He points out that another provision of the Motor Vehicle Code,

Section 27160, requires manufacturers to comply with a diminishing noise level depending on the year of manufacture. These are the maximum decibel levels allowed by law in California:

Motorcycle manufactured before January 1, 1970.....92

Motorcycle manufactured after January 1, 1970
and before January 1, 1973.....................88

Motorcycle manufactured on or after January 1, 1973..86

Motor-driven cycle manufactured after January 1,
1968, and before January 1, 1973................86

Motor-driven cycle manufactured on or after
January 1, 1973 84

What this means is that the owner of a 92-decibel motorcycle is expected to maintain it in 92 decibel condition. It also implies that all owners of motorcycles in California had better know how loud their street machines sound, because they may receive traffic citations. Not only that, but seven of the twenty-two proposals in Sacramento would revise the present standards to an even quieter level.

California has another law, Section 27150 of the Motor Vehicle Code, which requires a muffler on all registered motorcycles and leaves the enforcement of a provision against "unusual or excessive noise" pretty much up to the officer on the street. Sanford claims that this section has nailed many motorcyclists, who have been convicted in court even though their bikes met the requirements of Section 23130 (noise standards they must maintain) and Section 27160 (noise standards manufacturers must conform to).

Laws like this, which undoubtedly exist in other states, leave the motorcycle rider at the mercy of curbstone justice. In California one of the twenty-two bills in the hopper is designed to eliminate the injustice of the "unusual or excessive noise" rule. It would require that the California Highway Patrol conduct scientific tests upon which reasonable standards would be set in line with economic and engineering facts. Once these standards are established, if the bill becomes law, it would then be necessary for a police

Ecologists are down on off-road riders partly because of the way some of them litter. Unfortunately, not all motorcyclists are careful about where they dump their trash. Thoughtlessness such as this has made it tough on all off-road riders and has lined up hard core ecologists against the sport of motorcycling.

officer to prove scientifically that the motorcycle was too noisy rather than to stand there and listen to it and decide for himself.

It is certainly reasonable that noise standards be set and maintained on public streets and highways. Particularly in cities, traffic noise is said to be a contributing factor to poor mental health. Ecologists are now telling us that the same harmful effects of loud noise apply as well to wildlife. Excessive noise frightens animals and sometimes "disorients" them, that is confuses them and makes them forget where they are or what they were just about to do. It doesn't take too much imagination to predict that noise standards will be applied to off-road motorcycles in the near future. Bills to do just that have already been introduced in the California legislature, and one has passed.

The new law extends Section 27150 (the "unusual or excessive noise" law) to all off-road vehicles. The legislator who introduced it admitted he erred and has already proposed an amendment that would make the test of "unusual or excessive noise" any decibel level above those required for motorcycle manufacturers (Section 27160).

Both to conform with the new noise laws and also to live up to what are considered to be broad public responsibilities, the motorcycle industry is attacking the noise problem in its own way. On the retail level dealers will not sell an unmuffled motorcycle manufactured after December 1971. They coach their salesmen to do everything they can to discourage the sale of unmuffled expansion chambers and megaphones. At the factory level research is going on that will soon enable production motorcycles to put out maximum horsepower with the muffler intact. In addition, a new bike owner who tampers with his muffler risks having his warranty voided. At the racing level many clubs and associations require bikes with expansion chambers to be muffled as a condition of each entry.

The concept that wilderness areas are just as spoiled by noise as by littering, carelessness with fire, indiscriminate real estate development, plundering of natural resources and emission of water and air pollution is a new one, but it makes some sense. Rather than being unfairly restrictive of motorcycle activity, however, noise legislation for off-the-road vehicles will probably turn out to be a routine matter that riders will learn to live with. To enjoy the privilege of riding in areas where no other human sets foot, or at least where no other vehicles can travel, it is going to be necessary for motorcyclists to observe some simple restraints.

ECOLOGY

It used to be called conservation. In school we all studied about how the loggers and the oil drillers and the gold miners literally ripped apart some of the richest and most beautiful land in the United States to extract minerals, water power and lumber. To be in favor of conservation and against exploitation was something every youngster learned to do, but few were ever in a position to practice.

Today's ecologists give us all a guilty conscience. We are all to be blamed for damaging our environment by creating pollution, by littering, by allowing bad planning of suburban and rural areas and poor zoning practices in the cities, by our wanton destruction of plant and animal life and poor population planning. We can no longer blame only the big corporations for ruining our scenic open country. Every one of us is just as much at fault.

The off-road vehicle enthusiast is a convenient scapegoat for the ecologist and some cyclists deserve it. While the motorcyclist doesn't choke the seashore with tons of crude petroleum from leaking offshore drilling sites, he does occasionally start brush fires because his bike is not equipped with a spark arrester. He does leave litter behind. Some thoughtless riders rip through virgin brush country, crushing tender plants, or deliberately killing small animals and birds. Ecologists sensitive to the delicate balance of nature would rather motorcycles not be allowed in places where they could endanger the natural scheme of things.

As we pointed out before, noise pollution has become an important rallying point for those concerned with the preservation of other species of life on this planet. One of the early targets of ecologists was the snowmobile driver. Charging across the still, white countryside during hibernation periods of most animals, the snowmobilist was accused of waking and frightening the fauna of the land, disturbing their life cycles and threatening their extinction.

At other seasons the motorcyclist and the dune buggy driver are said to do almost the same thing. Therefore, there are those who would eliminate the sport of off-road motorcycling or at least severely restrict it. To preserve the right to ride in wilderness areas the motorcycle enthusiast must use good sense and restraint while moving about in nature's wonderland.

ENCROACHMENT

There is more than one use for open land. It is there not only to ride a motorcycle across. It attracts a great variety of nature loving people, who have many different reasons for being there. There are sportsmen, who hunt or fish. There are campers and hikers. There are prospectors and explorers. There are geologists and botanists. Some ranchers use public land to graze their livestock. There are homesteaders who either occupy the land to settle on it, to retire or to make use of it as a vacation retreat. Most of them resent interference with their own personal pursuits.

Folks who fled to the country to "get away from it all" do not like to wake up in the morning to the sound of loud motorcycles. Ranchers get boiling mad when arrogant motorcyclists trespass on their land, sometimes leaving gates open or cutting their way through fences. Fishermen are perturbed when cyclists splash through streams and frighten fish away. Destruction of crops and stealing or killing livestock often makes the motorcyclist who had nothing to do with the original crime an innocent target of vengeful farmers armed with guns. Once we wrote in a newspaper column about the need for more motorcycle recreation areas to satisfy the need for the off-road cyclist, and we were astounded by the amount of mail the column attracted—every letter against motorcycles. One retired gentleman who lives on a dirt road where young riders travel on weekends en route to the back country invited us to trade homes for a weekend to see how we liked the noise level he had to live with.

In California, the restriction of off-road motorcycling reached epidemic proportions in 1970 when four of the southern counties where most of the desert riding is done—Los Angeles, Orange, San Bernardino and Riverside—passed ordinances forbidding a rider to use private land without the owner's permission. Many cities also adopted anti-motorcycle ordinances that were so strict that a youngster could not even ride a minibike on his own front lawn legally.

The issue of pro- and anti-motorcycling never came more clearly in focus than it did in the Bean Canyon case. Bean Canyon is a scenic wonderland near Bakersfield, California, laced with motorcycle trails that have been in use for more than twenty years. Riders used to come from all over the West to enjoy the area. There was never a complaint until two things happened. Roger Nichols, a song writer for Herb Alpert, bought a parcel of land on top of a hill overlooking the canyon, and he began planning to build. Soon he became aware of the fact that motorcyclists were crisscrossing his property despite all the postings telling them to "keep out." One story goes that a fresh bike rider reached out and pinched Nichols's wife one day as she stood on her homesite. Meanwhile, the hillside was acquired by land speculators who subdivided it and began selling parcels to vacation home seekers and retired people. They were probably doing a far more damaging thing to the ecology of the area by cutting down trees and leveling building sites than the bike riders had by riding there, but salesmen objected strenuously to riders racketing back and forth, while they were trying to make their sales to elderly couples in search of a quiet mountain retreat.

One or more of the new property owners induced a local magistrate to take action against offending motorcyclists. So officers began appearing on the scene in January 1969. From then through April they stopped each rider, indicated they were taking a "survey" and wrote down the rider's name and address. Nearly everyone cooperated. Meanwhile, complaints were drawn up in April charging one hundred and fifty persons with violations of the state trespassing law, and these were served by mail in June and July. Many of the one hundred and fifty thought they were being cited for traffic violations and merely pleaded guilty. They were shocked to learn the fine was $65. Very few realized they were being charged with a misdemeanor for which they could serve time in jail. One rider wrote a letter to *Cycle News* telling of his predicament, and the letter brought response from many others who were charged with the same offense. An AMA District 37 official put the writer in touch with an enthusiastic Bakersfield motorcyclist who also happened to be a lawyer.

Attorney Ray Alan Yinger wound up representing sixty-five riders who had been served with the same complaint. All sixty-five cases were eventually dismissed on a legal technicality, which did not touch on the constitutional issue of the right of motorcyclists to use open land. Since October 1969, when the sixty-five cases were dismissed, California's trespass law has been tightened, and its validity has been upheld in lower courts. The law makes it a crime for a motor vehicle to be on private property without the owner's permission. Yinger and others believe the law has constitutional defects, but to date there has not been an appeal to test that theory.

USE OF PUBLIC LAND

The most enlightened government agency, from the point of view of the motorcycle enthusiast, is the Bureau of Land Management. The BLM, which for years has concerned itself mainly with administering the disposal of homestead land of the federal government, has suddenly found itself in the recreation business. The BLM administers 457 million acres of government land. The problem it has been asked to deal with is off-road vehicle use of open Western land under its control.

The concern is many-sided. Ranchers have grazing rights on some of the acreage. Ecologists are worried that off-road vehicles are permanently scarring the landscape. There are operators who indiscriminately drive wherever they please. Scientists complain that valuable fossils and archeological remains have been severely damaged by motorcycle, dune buggy and ATV drivers. Particularly in California, where desert motorcycle riders have been legally pushed off nearly everything else, there has been pressure to use BLM land for off-road vehicle recreation.

So the BLM appointed a group of affected citizens called the Off-Road Vehicle Advisory Committee (ORVAC) to study the problem. Its fifteen members represent ranchers, ecologists, the California Department of Fish and Game, and off-road vehicle users. Their main recommendation has already been put into effect.

ORVAC suggested that BLM land be classified into three uses. Class 1 is open, class 2 is restricted and class 3 is closed. Open use means that just about anything goes. Motorcyclists may use restricted land, but they must first obtain a permit. Each permit application is to be judged on its merit. A restricted area might have a high wildlife population, or it may be classified as such to protect the cyclist from such unusual hazards as mine shafts and excavations. Areas are classified permanently closed to protect historic sites, fossils and other priceless facets of the wilds in the West. It is sad to report that the great Indian Intaglios east of San Diego, California, have been all but destroyed by thoughtless and selfish off-road vehicle users.

The BLM has also recognized the so-called checkerboard problem which makes it impossible for riders to use vast areas under its control. There are many land owners in the desert, including the state but more particularly the railroads, which acquired tremendous amounts of acreage years ago. Checkerboarding, a plan also practiced by ranchers, involves acquiring every other section (square mile) of land. This makes for an impossible situation as far as the motorcycle rider is concerned.

In most of the affected areas there are local ordinances forbidding off-road riding on private property without the owner's permission. Under these ordinances and the new California trespass law, many motorcyclists have been cited for riding on BLM land. The officer merely hands the citation over to the rider and leaves it up to him to prove to a judge whether or not he was on private property. That's next to impossible. There are very few surveyor's stakes in the California desert.

The BLM has already helped to alleviate this situation by opening the first of what may be many desert recreation areas. It is located in Stoddard Valley, just south of Barstow, California, on 12,000 acres of what is described as a motorcyclist's paradise. There is every type of terrain from flat valleys to mountains in the parcel.

Soon the BLM hopes to have the authority to carry out the next phase of its program, which is to go into the land swapping business. By exchanging acreage with the owners of desert checkerboards, the BLM would open additional recreation areas. A bill to implement this plan was introduced in the U.S. House of Representatives in July 1971, by Congressman Bob Mathias of Tulare, California, the two-time Olympic decathlon champion. Called the California Desert Management Act, it would give the BLM acquisition authority and establish a long range program for management, development and use of public land under the jurisdiction of the BLM.

There are two other government agencies which control public land: the U.S. Forest Service, and the National Park Service.

There are 154 forest areas and 18 grasslands with a total area of 81 million acres administered by the U.S. Forest Service. National forests are visited by 12 million campers every year.

Most of the forest areas are closed to all riding except that which is done on designated roads and trails. Recently, an experiment has been tried in the Los Padres National Forest near Santa Barbara, California, in which bike riders using U.S. Forest Service-approved spark arresters are allowed to ride anywhere on a particular 75-acre parcel. Riders are on their good behavior, because if the experiment is successful—that is, if the land is not damaged by carelessness or vandalism—it will be opened permanently, and perhaps other national forests will be opened to riders as well.

The National Park Service has the strictest rules of all. It is charged with managing the priceless heritage of such natural wonders as Yellowstone, Brice, Zion, Yosemite and Glacier National Parks. Under its jurisdiction are thirty-two national parks, seventy-seven national monuments, six national seashores and four national recreation areas along with hundreds of historic sites. Riding in most parks is restricted to existing roads. Only in a few cases are motorcycles allowed on hiking and equestrian trails.

States have been slow to respond to the needs of their citizens for off-road vehicle recreation. Several have considered bills which would in effect license and register off-road vehicles and use the license revenue to acquire land and make improvements on it for motor vehicle recreation use. At this writing, none have been passed into law, but the chances of such an arrangement appear more likely every day.

The city of Los Angeles, which may have more motorcyclists than any other city in the world, has been particularly hard on off-road riding and has blocked several proposals to establish municipal riding areas. After closing an area near the black ghetto that had been used by youngsters on minibikes and small motorcycles for years, the City Recreation and Parks Department proposed in 1969 to open a riding area thirty miles north of the city near Newhall, California. The fact that poor minority children had been deprived of one more recreation opportunity and would be unable to take advantage of the new motorcycle park, if and when it is opened, apparently had little influence on the city officials. In all fairness, the riding area was closed in order to to preserve a bird sanctuary. Two years after city officials promised motorcycle enthusiasts they would replace the closed area with a municipal recreation facility there still was no bike park.

Meanwhile, in nearby Anaheim and Fullerton, California, two municipal riding areas were acquired by the recreation and park departments of those smaller cities, possibly the first two in the United States to provide its citizens with such facilities.

Into the void left by local government authorities, who have obviously either been reluctant to establish motorcycle parks, been unable to due to lack of funds or simply haven't considered the problem, have jumped the private entrepreneurs.

half-mile dirt racing
Ascot Park
Gardena, California

Ascot Park is the Mecca of motorcycle racers. Riders in a heat race are tightly bunched in the first turn.

Nineteen-year-old Keith Mashburn leans into a corner.

Head-on view of corner exiting technique. Note the various lines all four riders are taking, each trying to find the proper "bite" in the dirt for his machine.

Chuck Palmgren (#8) leads Gene Romero (#1), Eddie Mulder (#20) and two others through a half-mile turn.

Jim Rice (#2) takes advantage of a fast track, leading two others through a wide groove.

In Southern California alone there are a dozen motorcycle recreation parks which have become known to enthusiasts all over the country—Saddleback Park, Claude Osteen Bike Park, Indian Dunes Park, Escape Country, Muntz Cycle Park, to name a few. Most of them feature both riding trails and competition areas where regular motocross, hillclimb, scrambles and TT races are held. Expansion of the motorcycle recreation park business into a nationwide industry is easily predictable. In Japan Honda already has a network of these parks, and the company has encouraged their establishment all over the world.

AIR POLLUTION

Automobiles, trucks and buses have been singled out for attention by the lawmakers who are sensitive to the public's growing concern about the quality of the air we breathe. In the war on smog, it is only a matter of time before they will turn their attention to motorcycles.

It is too early to predict what form of restrictions will be imposed on motorcycle users, but the inevitability of smog control is too important to ignore. It is true that it takes the exhaust of five or six 250cc motorcycles to equal the output of a Volkswagen, but there is exhaust, the exhaust is probably dirty and eventually it will have to be cleaned up by government action.

THEFT

Theft of all motor vehicles is up to 20 percent in the United States, but theft of automobiles is down 27 percent. Obviously motorcycle owners are suffering. Motorycycles are being stolen at the rate of 150 per day. Insurance costs are rising even more rapidly than the rate of inflation, and even though higher rates are compensating for higher losses, insurance companies can't keep up with the thieves of today. Recently in Massachusetts and New Jersey the insurance companies were found to be paying out $2 for every $1 they were collecting. Other high loss states were Georgia, Nebraska and Texas. Police officials estimate that today's motorcycle owner has about a 25 percent chance of getting his bike back if it is stolen. In addition to young joyriders, who account for a high percentage of all stolen vehicles, very highly organized professional theft rings are in operation in various parts of the country. The problem of preventing theft and reclaiming stolen motorcycles has reached such proportions that authorities have moved to do something to help the motorcycle owner.

Federal highway safety regulations call for every new motorcycle sold to have a Vehicle Identification Number. These can be successfully altered by the professional criminal, who typically forges a bogus registration for the stolen bike by using the registration for a crashed motorcycle that lies in a junk yard somewhere. But the day is coming soon when these numbers will be quite difficult to tamper with. The Society of Automotive Engineers has appointed a Committee on Vehicle Security to study the problem, and the National Auto Theft Bureau is also studying the special motorcycle problem. Proposals they have already suggested include making the numbering system easier to understand, placing serial numbers at various places on the bike, including inside the engine, and underlaying the Vehicle Identification Number with a grid that would be damaged if anyone tried to alter it.

The time is not far off when some new owner protection system will become standard for the United States and probably Canada as well. Today, using the present system, Vehicle Identification Numbers are transmitted throughout the United States and into Canada twenty-four hours after a theft.

Police report that their biggest headache in locating stolen motorcycles is the mistakes owners make in reporting their own numbers. Often it isn't their fault, because errors are made by clerks who record the registration papers and because some dealers are just plain sloppy. One California dealer was recently fined $750 for incorrectly reporting the serial numbers of 250 motorcycles he had sold.

It isn't much consolation to the motorcyclist who has just had his bike lifted, but legislation is on its way to help make it tougher for professionals to succeed in their illicit business. Meanwhile, it would be a good idea to look at the ways you can help prevent theft of your own machine:

1 *Try to park where you can keep an eye on it.* If that isn't possible, the bike should be parked where it is well lighted or where somebody else can watch it, such as a parking attendant.

2 *Always lock the bike.* That isn't 100 percent protection, but it usually slows the thief down, and if you make it tough enough for him, he may give up altogether. The best type is a steering lock, but a padlock and chain wrapped around a solid object like a light standard or fence is also good insurance.

3 *Trick the thief.* Remove the spark plug and replace it with a non-working plug. Take an old, worn-out plug and deactivate it by breaking the electrode off the side. Put the phony in and carry the working plug away with you when you park. Or swap a dummy plug wire for the real one. You can often frustrate anyone but a seasoned pro by pulling tricks like these.

4 *Sound the alarm.* There are several good burglar alarms available, and you can rig your own by connecting the horn to the kick stand so that if the stand is disturbed, the horn goes off.

5 *Carry the Vehicle Identification Number.* It's too much to trust to memory, and often the only hope of recovering a motorcycle lies in quick reporting of the theft. Make sure, incidentally, that the number on the motorcycle registration is correct. Don't assume it is. Check the number.

TRAFFIC CITATIONS

No matter how careful a rider is, he may wind up in traffic court. Eighty-five percent of the time he will be guilty of some infraction and know it, 10 percent of the time he will be guilty of some violation of which he was ignorant until he collected the ticket, and the rest of the time he will be innocent.

Obviously, we are not interested in discussing the outcome of cases involving the guilty, even the "innocent" guilty who knew not what they did wrong until they got caught doing it. The law assumes everyone knows what is legal and what isn't. It is every citizen's responsibility to make himself informed. Let's discuss what to do in the case of a wrongful citation, the one instance in twenty that should result in acquittal or dismissal.

The first thing to consider in defending yourself is whether or not to retain a lawyer. It's to be expected that the defendant in a minor traffic case will pay out more to an attorney than he will if he merely pleads guilty and pays his fine. One thing a lawyer can do, however, is advise the client how to appear in court and what procedures to follow if he is going to represent himself. American justice is supposed to work in favor of the accused until he is found guilty—and even after that, until he has exhausted every avenue of appeal. But once a traffic violation suspect gets into court he finds it doesn't always operate that way. A good attorney will help his client take advantage of every possible break under the rules of the court. He can advise when it is a good idea to enter a *nolo contendere* (no contest) plea rather than guilty or not guilty, whether to have a jury trial, what type of evidence to collect, which judge to avoid because of hostile attitudes, which judge to seek out because of his reputation for fairness, how to question an arresting officer when he is on the stand, how to ask for a continuance and how to conduct one's self in front of the judge. In the case of the innocent, money for a lawyer is well spent, whether the attorney winds up making an actual court appearance or not.

The second thing to consider is the likelihood of perjury. All things being equal, a judge will be more likely to believe a police officer than a defendant, and the policeman knows that. It's only natural. However, the police officer approaches a court appearance somewhat differently from a man fighting a ticket. First of all, he probably had to come to court on his own time. That doesn't improve his humor any. Second, refusal to plead guilty is a challenge to his validity, possibly even to his honesty. That makes him grumpier and more determined to get a conviction. Third, it is impossible for every policeman to remember the details of every moving violation for which he writes a ticket. Some traffic officers deal out as many as twenty a day (even though they protest that there is no such thing as a quota system). To cover up for his lack of recall in comparison with that of the violator, who might remember the exact conversation between the two of them and have witnesses to back up his story, the policeman resorts to a pat sort of jargon, such as "I observed the defendant proceeding northbound in an erratic manner. . . ." Quite often attempts to get a police officer to correct his story through questioning are futile even though he has made an obvious misstatement. He has been to court enough times to know how to handle himself. He is not likely to offer anything that would be helpful to the defense.

The third element of preparation for a court hearing is the gathering of all helpful evidence and testimony that will get the defendant's story across to the judge. It is important to be thorough and not overlook anything. Recall the exact place where the officer began clocking or observing the defendant. What was he doing just before that? Note traffic and weather conditions. Did he say anything out of line? Talk to possible witnesses. Drive by the area again and look for traffic signs. Are they hidden, hard to see, damaged? Take photographs to back up any story. One friend of ours pleaded innocent to traveling 45 mph in a 35-mile zone, then went on the stand to testify he was indeed traveling 45—and won the case! First he went back to the place where he was stopped, along a route he traveled every day and knew well, and took motion pictures of the traffic flow at the exact time of day he had been ticketed. His movies proved that traffic was rushing by at 50 to 55 mph, and he managed to convince the judge that in traffic like that if he had gone any slower than 45 he would have been a hazard.

The fourth step is to pay careful attention to the presentation of the state's case. Take notes. The officer may make a misstatement or contradict himself. If the judge doesn't catch it, make sure you call it to his attention.

The fifth and perhaps the most important part of a successful defense is to make a good appearance before the judge. It may be surprising to learn that traffic court judges are pleased to hear an intelligent, logical defense and will lean sympathetically toward a person who is obviously sincere in his belief that he has been wronged. Judges however don't appreciate dirty clothes, skin or hair, foul language or disrespect in any form. He can see through an obvious attempt to put something over on him. His experience has taught him that nearly everybody who appears before him in traffic court is guilty, and this experience has to make him skeptical of your defense whether he wants to be fair or not. If he catches a police officer in an obvious lie, he will probably give him a tongue lashing right there in the courtroom in front of you. Or if he doesn't like the way either case is presented, he'll probably say so. He will look upon a shoddy defense as wasting his time. It is not unusual for a policeman to be suspended for a short period if he traps himself in court in the act of lying about a traffic ticket. That can hurt the officer in the wallet, and it is even more reason why you can't expect to get a fair shake out of the police officer when you go to court against him and you are right. We know a fellow who learned this lesson. After being acquitted on an unfair traffic charge, he found himself being followed every day for three months by a traffic officer.

"You should have seen me," he said. "I was driving like a minister."

The traffic court judge sees himself an an instrument for traffic safety. He believes he acts as a deterrent to highway deaths by levying fines, suspending licenses and ordering bad drivers to go to school. Maybe he does. At the very least he is entitled to the respect due a person who is trying to help society.

7

Let's Go Racing

Three riders went down, Jack Goulsen, Dick Klamfoth and J. C. Robertson. Right behind them, too close to swerve away from the tangle, came Carroll Resweber, his Harley-Davidson screaming as the cloud of dust swallowed him at 100 mph.

Three pieces of debris flew out of that cloud—two halves of the motorcycle tumbled down the track and Resweber rocketed into the infield fence. The accident stopped the race at Lincoln, Illinois, on September 16, 1962. Spectators jumped to their feet gasping. The greatest dirt track champion of all time, Carroll Resweber, was hurt badly, maybe even killed.

He might have died, except that a medic gave Resweber mouth to mouth resuscitation on the way to the hospital. Goulsen died in the same ambulance. Resweber's injuries were catastrophic. He had a broken neck, a right leg fractured in six places (it needed a cast for two years), a left arm so badly mangled that it would be eighteen months before he could move his fingers. It took Carroll Resweber, the 1958–59–60–61 American Motorcycle Association Grand National champion, a full month before he realized that the young woman visiting him daily in the hospital was his wife.

Resweber was the Babe Ruth, the Johnny Unitas, the Pelé, the Arnold Palmer of his sport. His name today? It has a hollow ring. The people in his hometown of Port Arthur, Texas, scarcely realize they have a celebrity living among them. Carroll Resweber Day was not celebrated there but in Cedarburg, Wisconsin, where the townspeople gave him a new automobile and paraded him through town.

Motorcycle racing, the sport which spawned Carroll Resweber, has had its share of boom and bust periods. Apparently entering another growth era today, its past is obscured by many years of struggle, during which great athletes like Resweber were not accorded the recognition of other superstars in more conventional sports. Great champions of the early days are not revered today like Jim Thorpe, Cy Young and Barney Oldfield. Whoever heard of Otto Walker, Joe Petrali, Carl Goudy and Ed Kretz? Perhaps a few old-timers have, but it is a shame that the rich heritage of motorcycle racing is practically lost to the modern generation of enthusiasts.

Motorcycle racing was born in 1896 with the first international event, the Emancipation Run, which celebrated the end of England's oppressive laws against motor vehicles. The following year France, which had originated automobile racing in 1887, held a motorcycle competition on the roads linking Paris with Dieppe. The sport had its early roots in the United States with the advent of "pacer" motorcycles that were used to block the wind for

A British speedway motorcycle racer shows the peculiar stand-up riding technique used with the fuelburning lightweight 500cc machines, which roar flat out around very short tracks, rather than accelerate and slow for the corners as the flat trackers do. Believe it or not, he is being photographed from the infield and is moving from right to left, turning left.

bicycle racers around the turn of the century. Informally the pacer riders got together and staged races of their own.

George Hedstrom, developer of the Indian motorcycle, gambled that the success of his bike in the marketplace would follow racing victories. In 1902 Hedstrom organized the first factory team in United States history. Indian won a race, a hillclimb and an endurance run, assuring the marque of an instant reputation. In 1906 Hedstrom took an Indian to the speed trials at Ormond Beach, Florida, and raced Alexander Winton's famed race car, "Bullet." Hedstrom placed second in a handicap match, covering the flying mile at an average speed of 68.3 mph, but "Winton never did actually pass me," Hedstrom said later.

In 1909 an Indian was raced in the Isle of Man TT, and the American motorcycle was represented in that race every year year afterward through 1923.

Racing in the United States evolved into a dirt track sport in the early 1900s, while in Europe the emphasis was on road racing. International competition began in 1905, when France invited each nation to send a three-man team. The British held a runoff to choose the team on the mystic Isle of Man, using public roads on the island, but their three-man team lost the Paris event to a Frenchman. The next year they also lost the international race held in Austria to an Austrian rider amid charges that he was illegally helped by two accomplices on a sidecar rig. When the winner wasn't disqualified, Britain decided to withdraw from racing on the continent.

Thus the stage was set for the first race on the Isle of Man, modestly called the Tourist Trophy. The Marquis de Mouzilly St. Mars, a friend of the Collier family which built the Matchless, donated the trophy, which was a copy of one that had been struck a few years earlier for an automobile race over the same roads. On a cold, breezy day the 28th of May, 1907, twenty-five riders were flagged off two at a time. Ten finished, with Charlie Collier the winner on a Matchless at 38.22 mph and 94.5 miles per gallon.

In the years that followed, the race course grew tougher and longer through addition of roads through the rugged mountains, while the prestige of winning took on international proportions. Although today there is an international championship for road racing in many engine classes, contested in ten separate countries, the Isle of Man Tourist Trophy stands alone as the premiere event in the world.

Some of the race's mystique stems from the unusual heritage of the island, inhabited by fiercely independent but superstitious people who have remained unspoiled by the outside world for more than 1000 years. Folk legends of the Middle Ages survive today in the lore of the island people to torment riders on the 37.75-mile mountain course.

The race starts on the approach to Bray Hill, which leads to the town of Douglas. Just beyond Douglas stands the roofless church of St. Trinians, now in ruins alongside the sharp turn onto the road that leads to Ballacraine. As the story goes, one of the island's evil spirits, called a Buggane, took hideous pleasure in tearing the roof off the church each time it was completed. One night a brave tailor named Timothy volunteered to stand watch over the church, but soon after he had sat down in the field to finish stitching a suit the Buggane rose out of the ground. The tailor put in the

MERT LAWWILL – 6th Ranked AMA Racer/Houston, Texas Short Track Champion; Cumberland, Maryland Half-Mile Champion; Gardena, California T. T. Champion.

JIM RICE – 2nd Ranked AMA Racer/Houston, Texas T. T. Champion; Palmetto, Georgia Half-Mile Champion; Reading, Pennsylvania Half-Mile Champion; San Jose, California Half-Mile Champion; Santa Rosa, California Mile Champion; Peoria, Illinois T. T. Champion.

final stitch and fled for the church, as the Buggane ripped off the roof and threw it at him. The roof missed Timothy just as he reached sacred ground, where no harm could befall him. The Manx have left the church unfinished to this day, and an old pair of scissors purported to be Timothy's are on display at a local inn.

Beyond the ruined building is Greeba Mill, where the Dark River provides a sanctuary for a water bull called Tarro-Ushtey. Tarro-Ushtey has a sweet tooth for tender calves, and farmers used to find piles of hair by the river in place of their livestock.

At Ballacraine the riders turn north through a tricky, twisting section known as Ballig-Glen Helen. Beyond Birkin's Bend, where Archie Birkin was killed in 1927 when he ran into a van while practicing, the riders pass Bishopscourt. There the bishop of Sodor and Man looked out over the countryside from his thirteenth century tower. On a farm nearby lives one of the good spirits, called a Phynoderee. To help the farmer build his house, the kindly elf brought boulders from the seacoast at night and laid them in place.

Just before the 24-mile mark, Ramsey, a landmark known as Clover Hill is the last meeting place of the witches, who on the evening of every May 11 used to light fires on top of the hill. At the bottom of the hill spinsters marched and sang on the night

GARY NIXON – 10th Ranked AMA Racer/Loudon, New Hampshire Road Race Champion.

EDDIE MULDER – 20th Ranked AMA Racer/Hinsdale, Illinois T. T. Champion.

CHUCK PALMGREN – 8th Ranked AMA Racer/Nazareth, Pennsylvania Mile Champion.

MARK BRELSFORD – 7th Ranked AMA Racer/Oklahoma City Half-Mile Champion.

of Good Friday to announce they were in need of husbands.

Ramsey is the most northern corner of the course, which winds its way around much of the island that measures thirty-three miles from north to south and twelve miles at its widest east–west point. Above Ramsey is Sky Hill, which in 1076 was the scene of a historic battle between the Manx and invading Norsemen. Sky Hill is the home of the island's fairies, who are said to have a city on its summit.

Past Ramsey is the mountain section. To the right, as the riders roar by at some of their highest speeds, is Carraghan Mountain, where the island's spinning lady lived. She was Ben Veg Carraghan, who was followed wherever she went by a great goose. Whenever she wanted to travel to the next mountain she curled herself into the spinning wheel, rolled down the mountain and right up the next one.

Coming out of the mountains, riders swoop into a valley where friendly Phynoderee have their home, Creg-ny-Baa. At night it is said they harvest the farmer's corn for him. But less than a mile farther, at the Governor's Bridge, dwells the spirit of the headless man, who haunts the road at night.

Although it was conceived as an English riding event, it did not take long for the Isle of Man TT to attract international attention.

In 1911, the Indian team of O. C. Godfrey, C. B. Franklin and A. J. Moorhouse completed the first 1-2-3 sweep in the senior race, a feat that wasn't equaled in ten years.

In 1962 Mrs. Beryl Swain competed in the 50cc race and finished 22nd. After this accomplishment Women's Lib suffered a blow; women were promptly barred from competition.

In a typical week of activity the riders cover more than 2800 laps, equivalent to 105,000 miles or nearly half the distance to the moon. Riders now compete on a variety of courses in nine separate races.

In 1903 a group of ninety-two American enthusiasts met in Brooklyn, New York, representing the New York and Alpha Motorcycle Clubs. They formed the Federation of American Motorcyclists, the forerunner to the American Motorcycle Association. Of the original group, forty-four agreed to kick in $2 apiece, and that served as their treasury.

In the United States two distinct types of professional racing evolved—dirt track and board track racing. Early dirt track racing was rough, no-holds-barred competition. Today the talk is about how flat track riders "lean on" each other but in early races they engaged in "hooking" contests in an effort to throw the rival down. It was during one of those hooking bouts between Charlie Balke and a great star of the day, Jake (The Fox) DeRozier, at Los Angeles, in 1912, that DeRozier went down at 90 mph. He was knocked unconscious, and his leg was so badly broken that doctors could never mend it. After a series of leg operations DeRozier died a few months later.

In 1913 Carl Goudy rode an Excelsior around the Columbus (Ohio) Driving Park for 100 miles in ninety-two minutes. He covered the distance eight minutes faster than Ralph de Palma did in an automobile a week later at Brighton Beach, New York. It was only the first of many important marks motorcyclists set during the period that came to be known as the Golden Era.

Such feats excited adventurous young men like Ralph Hepburn, a dispatch rider from Los Angeles who learned his racing trade both on the dirt and board tracks before World War I; Gene Walker, another delivery boy from Birmingham, Alabama; and Otto Walker, a mechanic who was later to set a board track

TOM ROCKWOOD – 9th Ranked
AMA Racer.

DON CASTRO – 5th Ranked AMA
Racer.

record of 100 miles at over 100 mph (101.431) that remains in the record books today.

The war intervened, but after the Armistice both forms of the sport blossomed. The first great flat track race was a 200-mile track championship, pitting the Harley-Davidson "wrecking crew" of Hepburn, Red Parkhurst, Al (Shrimp) Burns and Ray Weishaar against the Indian team of Bill Church, Dave Kinney, Bob Newman and Ralph Sullivan and the Excelsior team of Wells Bennett and M. Tice. Hepburn won with an average speed of 72.2 mph. By 1928 flat track racing was attracting crowds of 76,000 (at Syracuse, New York) who watched the three giants of America's motorcycle industry battle it out.

Even more spectacular was the rise of the board track motordrome. They were fairly common by 1912. At first the board tracks were short, wide and steeply banked, giving them the appearance of bowls. Each large city had a motordrome and its own team composed of a captain and three riders. The teams traveled a circuit the way professional baseball and football teams do, and the press not only reported the standings of the teams but also the winning "averages" of the individual riders which were worked out like baseball batting averages are today.

Wells Bennett, a leading rider of the day, recalled how things were:

DAVID ALDANA – 3rd Ranked AMA Racer/Talladega, Alabama Road Race Champion; Terre Haute, Indiana Half-Mile Champion; Indianapolis, Indiana Mile Champion.

DICK MANN – 4th Ranked AMA Racer/Daytona, Florida Road Race Champion; Castle Rock, Washington T. T. Champion.

Those dromes should not be confused with the rickety contraptions seen today in amusement parks and carnivals. The dromes were permanent structures of one-quarter or sometimes one-third mile in circumference. The surfaces were of pine two-by-two boards, and they were banked anywhere from 35 degrees to the daddy of them all at St. Louis, which had a 62-degree banking. Spectators had a view from seats ringing the top of the big pine bowl, with crowds of 5000 to 10,000 at the weekly races.

The ported engines were just coming out in 1912, and with speeds up to 90 per rolling against the steep banks put pressures of 700 pounds per square inch on the tires and 1500 pounds on the frame and axles. So if you unloaded, you would hit the planks a lot harder than in a flat track spill. A slide to the bottom could put 100 slivers in your anatomy. And if everything held together an overheated engine could burst into flames anytime.

The surface (of the board tracks) could not be planed off, or the coating of oil that spewed out of those open port engines (about a half gallon every twelve miles) would have made them hopelessly slippery. Every six weeks the whole track was washed down with a strong lye and water solution. This restored the traction for those two-inch smooth tread Goodyear special tires we used. These were pumped up to 100 pounds per square inch.

We had a hand pump on the side of the gas tank in addition to the oil pump in the engine, and every lap we gave the engine a shot of oil. This blew out of the cylinder ports in a fog that saturated the clothing of the riders and prevented our wearing goggles, which would fog up and become useless. At speeds up to and over 90 mph, tears would fill the eyes, but to make matters worse, after the lye bath on the track some of this irritant would be carried into the eyes, and the tears would flow freely back over our ears in the wind stream, but it did keep the eyes washed out to some extent.

One of the most serious hazards was the typical Midwestern electrical storm, which could put a transformer out of commission in the neighborhood, blacking out the arena. As Bennett put it, "We circled a quarter-mile drome in about ten seconds, and many times we rode wheel to wheel. Even five seconds of darkness could cause a near disaster if one rider got out of line."

There were many spills, but few injuries. Riders of that day, when they fell off, limped over to another motorcycle, jumped on and rejoined the race. The only tragic mishap of the period occured in Cincinnati, when Odin Johnson flew off the edge of the track into the spectator seats. His gas tank exploded, killing him and seven others and injuring seventy persons.

As the Germans went on the march in World War I, it was almost as if someone had flipped a switch. Spectators stopped attending motordromes, and the unusual sport died quietly. Meanwhile, however, larger outdoor board tracks were flourishing both in motorcycle and auto racing. Riders were able to record fantastic speeds, and they attracted huge crowds. The biggest motorcycle race ever held up to that time was the race on September 12, 1915, on a two-mile board track at Chicago. Hometown favorite Carl Goudy sped to victory at 85.71 mph and won the $1000 purse.

Red Parkhurst won the last big event before the United States entered the war, on the two-mile track at Sheepshead Bay, Brooklyn, averaging 91.19 mph in 1916. He came back a few months later and set a twenty-four-hour endurance record on the same track, completing 1452.75 miles despite having to wait out rainstorms lasting three and a half hours.

By comparison with today's motorcycle performances, speeds recorded on the board tracks then may not seem so spectacular, but for the equipment available then the sustained high speeds were remarkable. One of Joe Petrali's three records still on the books is his ten-mile run at Laurel, Maryland, in 1925. Petrali, alone on a motorcycle, traveled 111.1 mph. For comparison, that year at Indianapolis Leon Duray set a new qualifying record in a Miller of 113.196 mph. The most amazing of all the board track records, also held by Petrali, was 100 miles at 100.3 mph set at Altoona, Pennsylvania, on July 4, 1925.

Curley Loomis also made history on August 21, 1926, with one lap around the 1¼-mile banked oval at Salem, New Hampshire, at 120.3 mph to become the first man ever to travel faster than two miles a minute on an oval with a motorcycle. The land speed record for a flying mile at that time was only 119.3 mph.

Board track racing was fashionable during the 1920s and drew a "carriage trade" type of audience. Tracks flourished almost until the stock market crash of 1929, but the disappearance of board tracks could have been predicted from the beginning. Board tracks were expensive to build and expensive to care for. They were usually built away from populated areas, but often as soon as they were built homes sprang up nearby, causing taxes and real estate values to go up. The last two tracks to go were at Altoona and Salem.

In 1913 the long distance desert race came into vogue with the inaugural San Diego-to-Phoenix race. It featured the great Cannonball Baker against Paul Derkum, Roy Artley, Joe Wolter and Harry Crandal. Derkum won the first one at an average speed of 30 mph. Practicing for the 1914 race, Paul Frantzen became stranded and nearly died.

Thrown off his bike, Frantzen was catapulted over a sand bank and partly buried in the slide that followed. His buried motorcycle was useless, so Frantzen took off on foot. Under a burning sun he dragged across the desert until sand seeping into his shoes made his feet raw, forcing him to throw away his shoes. At dark he fell asleep, but he awoke that night to the sound of cattle. Crawling toward the sound, he found Mexican guerrillas (these were the days of Pancho Villa) camped and tending their stolen cattle. The Mexicans gave him some water while they debated whether or not to kill him, finally put him on a horse and took him to within walking distance of a railroad station. Such were the hazards of early desert racing.

In England in 1907, the same year the first Tourist Trophy race was held, the famed high speed Brooklands track was opened at Weybridge. Many auto and motorcycle racing greats performed there until Brooklands fell silent with the start of World War II, later to be torn up to make way for a housing development. In April 1912 a young English rider, A. J. Moorhouse, lost control of his Indian on the railway straight, careened off the track and hit a telegraph pole with such impact that his goggle frames left imprints in the wood. He was killed instantly. The motorcycle was buried at the foot of that pole, in the same tradition that "Babs" was planted in the Pendine Sands after the death of her colorful driver, Parry Thomas. All the top racers at Brooklands were riding

BART MARKEL – 32nd Ranked AMA Racer/Hinsdale, Illinois, Short Track Champion.

GENE ROMERO – Grand National Champion/Sedalia, Missouri Mile Champion; Sacramento, California Mile Champion; Gardena, California Half-Mile Champion.

American motorcycles by 1921, including the famed Bert Le Vack on an Indian and Claude Temple and Douglas Davidson on Harley-Davidsons.

In the 1930s motorcycle racing developed a superstar, Ed Kretz. Kretz was a 180-pound hay truck driver living in Pomona, California, when he started racing in the mid-1930s. Before his racing days were over twenty-five years later he had won eleven AMA nationals, including two at Daytona, where he led the race fourteen times. He was still racing when his son, Ed Kretz, Jr., became an AMA star.

In the 1938 Laconia 200 Kretz fell off once, spent fifteen minutes in the pits repairing a carburetor, lost his left footboard and had to hold his boot up the final fifty miles. He gripped the bars so hard he wore through three layers of skin. But he won the race, finishing four laps in front, and turned the last lap faster than the first.

In the early days Kretz said he often won more money finishing second than he did winning because the winner had to spring for drinks. Becoming a stunt rider for the movies, Kretz developed a trick riding routine that he performed at fairs and carnivals on the weekends he wasn't racing. The veteran rider's final fling came at a 100-miler at Carrell Speedway in Los Angeles at the age of forty-three, when he not only won but lapped the great Joe Leonard, who finished second.

For his day in motorcycle racing, Leonard was the closest to being a superstar the AMA had. As a youngster he ran away from home in San Diego, California, with an old suitcase and $21 in cash. His object: To go racing. In Leonard's first year of competition he was national amateur champion. In his first year as an expert Leonard was runner-up to Bill Tuman. Then Leonard was champion in 1954, 1956 and 1957 and runner-up in 1958, 1960 and 1961 before turning all his attention to auto racing.

The AMA's Grand National title was conferred on the winner of the Springfield, Illinois, national from 1946 through 1953, when a point system was devised. The point system has been changed twice, but it is in effect today to evaluate the performances of hundreds of riders and to select from among them the most diversified talent of any two-wheel championship awarded in the world. The AMA Grand National circuit includes short track races, races on half-mile and mile dirt ovals, TT steeplechases on the dirt, and road races on the asphalt, calling for a variety of racing abilities.

Fortunately for present-day stars, the national champion is recognized more widely outside his sport than ever before. Mert Lawwill is one of the stars of a feature length documentary film on motorcycling, "On Any Sunday." Gary Nixon's biography has been published. Dick Mann, Bart Markel and Gene Romero are names more frequently seen in newspapers and heard over the radio. Stars like Jim Rice, Dave Aldana, Skip Van Leeuwen, Yvon du Hamel, Mark Brelsford, Tom Rockwood, Don Castro, Jodie Nicholas, Chuck Palmgren, Cal Rayborn, Don Vesco and Eddie Mulder are becoming familiar names in the media. Races are seen more frequently on national television. About a half dozen of the top riders are said to earn incomes in excess of $50,000 a year. It's not out of the question that some day a break between innings of a World Series game might be filled with a commercial showing a motorcycle rider knocking "greasy kid stuff" or giving a sales pitch for a razor blade.

The sudden interest in motorcycle racing is no accident. It is

Gene Romero is congratulated for winning the 1970 AMA Grand National riding championship by a well-wisher who pours a bottle of champagne over his head in the winner's circle at Sacramento, California.

the work of smart promoters who have put their minds to the problem of what to do to popularize the sport to take advantage of more and more motorcycle sales. The eye-opener was the success of the first race at the Houston Astrodome in 1968. Following that success promoter Don Brymer staged a series of very popular races in places like Madison Square Garden, Roosevelt Raceway and Arlington Park. The Brymer formula was expected to be followed closely in 1972, when several AMA nationals were proposed for horse racing tracks around the country.

At the same time superspeedways have come into the motorcycle racing picture. For years the road race with great prestige has been the Daytona Speed Week, using part of the high banked tri-oval along with a road course through the infield of Daytona International Speedway. Daytona promoter Bill France poured thousands of dollars into motorcycle racing when it wasn't profitable. In 1970, soon after the opening of France's newer and larger high banked track, Alabama International Motor Speedway at Talladega, Alabama, a 200-mile national championship race series was inaugurated there. It was followed by an inaugural national on the 2½-mile tri-oval at Pocono, Pennsylvania, and finally big time motorcycle racing arrived at the showcase of motor sport, Ontario Motor Speedway. In cooperation with Champion Spark Plug Company, Ontario staged the richest American motorcycle event ever held, with a guaranteed purse of $50,000 plus lap and accessory money sending the total purse to well over $100,000.

It is only a matter of time before the other great arenas of the nation open their gates to AMA national competition. It's not out of the question to think of dirt track races at Hialeah, Santa Anita and Churchill Downs, while road races are launched at Watkins Glen, Riverside, Elkhart Lake and Laguna Seca.

If there is any doubt about the future of motorcycle racing, one needs only to look to Europe for direction. In the international arenas of road racing, crowds of 50,000 and more are the rule rather than the exception. Motorcycle road races on the world championship circuit are held at famed auto racing courses like the German Nürburgring and Hockenheim, Spa-Francorchamps in Belgium and Monza in Italy. Also on the circuit are some of the most demanding left-and-right-turn courses on the continent, including Montjuich in Spain, Dundrod in Ireland, Sachsenring in East Germany and Brno in Czechoslavakia.

Motorcycle road racing has made a household name of Italy's national hero, Giacomo Agostini. Young, handsome and flamboyant, Agostini is the Joe Namath of Europe. He is sought for endorsements, roles in motion pictures and public appearances, but he lives a quiet life testing motorcycles at Maranello, hunting at Lake Iseo, driving a fast touring car or secluded in his bachelor pad. Ago, as he is known to his fans, has so far spurned the offer by Enzo Ferrari of a place on his auto racing team. Ferrari has tested Agostini in a racing car and declared him a natural driving talent. In 1971 Agostini wrapped up his sixth straight 500cc world championship and his fourth straight 350cc title. All ten are records. Mike Hailwood and Carlo Ubbiali had each won nine world championships, but neither of them have dominated international racing to the extent Agostini has.

In Europe there are three other forms of international competition with great prestige, motocross, speedway and the International Six Day Trials.

Motocross racing began in England in 1924 but didn't begin to gain popularity until after World War II. English riders were imported to France by a Paris promoter, who staged events in the late 1940s for his entertainment starved countrymen. Counting the appearance fees and prize money they won—and a lively business they conducted on the French black market—the Britons did well indeed. One of their more profitable stunts was to fill extra oil cans with butter, which was cheap in England but rationed in France, and sell them to restaurateurs. Scarce motorcycle parts were fair game as well. The importer for Matchless complained at one time that he hadn't been able to get a bike to sell for two years, while there were twenty French riders competing on them.

The first international championship, called the European championship, was awarded in 1952. It was upgraded to world status in 1957. In the years that followed, motocross' world championship trial grew to as many as seventeen races, all in different countries, but the FIM later restricted the number to twelve. They are held on both sides of the Iron Curtain—in Spain, France, Belgium, Yugoslavia, Italy, the USSR, Poland, Great

road racing

A rider falls in heavy traffic in the middle of a tight turn at Daytona International Speedway, while the other racers take a wide line to avoid hitting him.

Former champion Mert Lawwill concentrates on a turn aboard his streamline road racing machine.

Long lens camera bunches the field at a dirt track oval race. Riders have just come off a turn on a one-mile track and are heading down the straightaway, where they will accelerate to speeds of 115 mph.

Two riders collide and hit the dirt.

dirt track racing

moto-cross racing

Two riders duel on a down-hill jump.

The usual large field strings out behind the master, Malcolm Smith.

Clearing a mud hazard.

Britain, Finland, East Germany, Switzerland and Austria. In 1971 the first U.S. Grand Prix for Motocross, billed as the forerunner to a world championship race on this side of the Atlantic, was held in Carlsbad, California, with Sylvain Geboers of Belgium winning. It was believed that a world championship event might be awarded to this country in 1972.

At about the same time motocross was gaining international stature, a California promoter, Frank Cooper, was organizing desert races as a means of selling his off-road bikes—they were something of a novelty at the time. In 1951 he originated the Catalina race, a rugged event held on the barren island (owned at the time by P. K. Wrigley) twenty miles off the California coast from the Port of Los Angeles. The race was a great success while it lasted, with as many as 200 riders competing, but eventually residents of the island put a stop to it. Rough terrain events remained in the amateur status, known only to a few enthusiasts and competitors for many years until 1966 when a promoter brought Torsten Hallman of Sweden to America for exhibitions. This was the inspiration for the Trans-AMA series that originated in 1970. Meanwhile, motocross racing has grown in popularity at a fantastic rate. In Southern California, where interest is highest, there are summer weekends on which as many as 1500 riders are competing at eight separate locations on the same day.

Class A speedway racing originated in Australia and soon spread to England. It also arrived in Los Angeles during the Depression and proved to be a popular nighttime diversion. The early tracks were lighted baseball diamonds, which the promoters used to plow up to build tracks of about one-eighth mile. Intimacy with the riders was achieved by placing the track very close to the spectators.

A speedway track in an industrial section of Los Angeles was followed by others in San Diego, Long Beach, Sacramento, Emeryville, Fresno, Bakersfield, Santa Ana and San Francisco, and from there the sport spread to cities in New York, Illinois, Wisconsin, New Jersey and Connecticut. Speedway racing at one time reached Mexico City, where parimutuel betting was tried.

One American rider, Sprouts Elder, campaigned in Australia and came back to Los Angeles riding Australian style, which got him around the track much faster than anybody else. One night, in street clothes, he put on an exhibition and from then on was the star attraction in speedway racing for two years, until the other riders caught on to the style and began beating him. Soon riders were making $75 to $100 a night and racing on a circuit that took them to a different city every night of the week.

Seeing speedway races at a track at Loyola University of Los Angeles, Dominick (Peewee) Distarce got the idea for originating a new kind of race car. He gathered a number of enthusiasts and they all built miniature race cars using motorcycle and outboard engines for power. These were called "midgets" and first ran on the same Loyola track (now the athletic field at Loyola High School) that the speedway motorcycles used. Other enthusiastic spectators in those days were actors Clark Gable and Hoot Gibson.

In 1933 the California Highway Patrol staged the "National Short Track Championships" in the Los Angeles Memorial Coliseum, which had just been used the year before for the Olympic Games. Winner of the title was Cordy Milne, a Pasadena, California, youth. Cordy and his brother Jack toured Australia in 1935, where they developed their talent out of necessity.

"We had to win," Jack Milne recalled later. "It was a long swim

This is a partial view of the 2500 participants in a hare and hound race on the desert near Barstow, California. The line of starters was nearly one mile long. Cross-country desert races like this, although not all of them with as many riders, are held on every weekend in the West.

home. We had spent our last cent on the boat trip. When we saw a hole during a race we went through. All we had to lose was our lives."

Jack Milne won the Australian championship in 1936, and an Aussie promoter took them to England for team racing. Jack was on one team and Cordy on another, and there was actually talk for a time that the Milne brothers should be deported because they were depriving English riders of making a living.

In 1936 Cordy Milne finished fourth in the world championship finals and Jack seventh. The following year they teamed with another rider from their hometown of Pasadena, Lammy Lamoreaux, to score an unprecedented sweep. Jack, Cordy and Lammy finished one-two-three in the world championship.

In 1938 Jack Milne finished runner-up in the world championship, and Lamoreaux was third. The following year Cordy Milne was leading in points with three days to go before the world championship race in September when the Germans invaded Poland, war was declared and the race was off.

After World War II, speedway racing resumed in England, soon spread throughout Europe, but in the United States it failed to generate interest when it was tried again in Los Angeles between 1946 and 1949. Speedway racing didn't make a real comeback until 1967. The following year the Milne brothers, Jack and Cordy, opened a track in Costa Mesa, California, and their success has encouraged the spread of speedway racing to a dozen tracks around the United States.

One of the oldest and most demanding of all motorcycle events is the International Six Day Trials, which was started in England in 1913 and resumed in 1920. Except for war years it has been held every year since.

The United States has never won an I.S.D.T. title, but Americans came closest in 1971. The United States finished fourth to Czechoslovakia, West Germany and East Germany and might have won but for the engine failure suffered by Dick Burleson of the trophy team. The trials cover 1000 miles and consist of a series of timed events, endurance and special tests. The thirty-one American riders participating in 1971 took home a total of eleven gold medals and nine silver medals.

Sweden's Olle Petersson
in the Spanish Grand Prix
of Moto-cross.

The ultimate in motorcycle speed events is the Land Speed
Record. Motorcycle land speed records were not formally organized as early as the international speed records for automobiles.
Before 1920, when the Federation Internationale Motocycliste
began recognizing speed marks, records were poorly kept.

The earliest record of an officially timed run is credited to Glenn
Curtiss, 67.4 mph on a machine of his design at Ormond Beach,
Florida in 1904. Curtiss was clocked unofficially on the same
beach course at 136.364 mph in a V8 prototype of unknown displacement in 1907, when the absolute record for a four-wheel
vehicle was only 127.66 mph, set the year before by Fred Marriott
in the steam-powered "rocket." Trying to go faster in 1907, Marriott nearly killed himself in a spectacular crash. Curtiss, the
aviation pioneer, did not see his clocking bettered by an automobile until René Thomas of France recorded a flying kilometer of
143.31 mph in 1924—seventeen years later.

Neither the 68 mph mark of a German named Liese on an NSU
Twin in 1908, the 77.06 mph by Otto Lingenfelder, also on an
NSU, in 1909, the 94.92 mph of Matchless factory executive
Charlie Collier on a V Twin in 1910, nor any of the tremendous
speeds achieved by Americans on the board tracks had any official
status. It wasn't until 1920 that the FIM set up the machinery to
recognize world records, and the first to establish an "official" mark

was Eugene Walker of the United States, riding an Indian 61 of 1000cc displacement. He was the first man to break 100 mph officially when he was clocked at 103.77 at Daytona Beach, Florida, on April 14, 1920. He held the record for three years, but no other American found his way into the world record books for another thirty-six years.

English and German manufacturers engaged in a duel for international recognition through use of the Land Speed Record, much the way early automobile manufacturers had done before them. Claude Temple, Bert LeVack and J. S. Wright of England, riding 1000cc bikes, finally were outdistanced by Ernst Henne of the BMW factory with first a supercharged 750 bike and then a supercharged 500. Due to the interruption of World War II, Henne was the record holder for eighteen of the next twenty-one years, and when his prewar mark of 173.880 mph was broken it took another German to turn the trick.

Wilhelm Herz returned from the war to find the NSU factory a pile of rubble from allied bombings. Digging through the ruins, he found the rusted remains of his prewar racing bike, took it home and rebuilt it. He won several races with it, and when the motorcycle racing unit was reactivated Herz was hired by NSU. One of the first things he did was talk management into letting him try for the world speed record, which at the time was just shy of three miles a minute (180 mph). On April 12, 1951 Herz roared down the Munich Autobahn two ways to record a speed of 180.090 mph.

Five years later the record came to America, where it has remained. Johnny Allen (214.400), Jess Thomas (214.470), Bill Johnson (230.269) and Bob Leppan (245.667) raised it four times in the next ten years with Triumphs. Leppan did it with a radical streamliner that featured a high tail fin which was ridiculed by experts ("decorative" was the description of one journalist) but which has become standard on all Land Speed Record vehicles. Designer Alex Tremulis proved that the fin was needed to keep the bullet-shaped streamliners from acting like what they looked like—bullets—and rolling over.

In 1970 three riders were at the salt flats to go after the record and to surpass 250 mph. Don Vesco did it on a Yamaha at 251.924. Cal Rayborn took the salt next for a frustrating two weeks during which he rolled once at 100 mph when a retractable outrigger failed to work. But his computer-designed Harley-Davidson Sportster turned 265.492 mph on October 16, 1970, adding 14 mph to the record only one month after it had been set.

Competition for motorcyclists exists in great variety and at all skill levels. There are many kinds of endurance, speed, acceleration and skill events available to the novice as well as the professional of varying skills. Let's take a look at some of them:

AMATEUR COMPETITION

ENDUROS—They began in 1924 under AMA auspices as the National Six Day Trials. This was a road event that started in Cleveland, Ohio, and continued on the move through Toledo, Detroit, South Bend, Indianapolis, Louisville, Lexington, Cincinnati, Dayton, Columbus, Wheeling, Pittsburgh, Youngstown, Akron and back to Cleveland. Today's enduro is a non-speed event over many types of ground. Riders must maintain a certain average speed while crossing mountains, streams, sandpits, uneven land strewn with rocks, swamps and mud. Distances vary from 20 to 400 miles.

RELIABILITY RUN—Another non-speed event is run over regular roads, either dirt or paved, and over ground that could be traveled by automobiles.

TRIALS—A very low speed event, trials test the skill of a rider over a twisting obstacle course. Obstacles include water, rocks, fallen trees, steep hills and wooded or brush covered terrain.

RALLIES—The objective is to reach a destination as close to the allotted time as possible, using a set of instructions for average speeds and the route to travel which is not known until the rider is ready to start the event.

SCRAMBLES—A race over a closed course of one-half to two miles in length that has been graded. It usually includes a jump.

MOTOCROSS—Similar to a scrambles, its course may be longer than two miles but seldom less than a half mile. The difference is that a motocross course is simply laid out and is not graded. It is planned in such a way that it may have several jumps, water and mud hazards and usually tricky up and downhill sections.

HARE AND HOUND—This is a cross-country race, very popular in desert areas, where several hundred riders have been known to start an event. The Big Bear Run, since discontinued, had 800 riders entered annually. Dan Gurney was a participant in that event before he went to Europe to become a grand prix driver.

HARE SCRAMBLES—A race of a number of laps over a meandering desert course usually about ten miles long.

ICE RACING—Found in the north country, particularly in Canada, it is racing over an oval course staked out on a frozen lake. It is extremely dangerous, since riders use special tires with spikes in them to grip the ice. Falling down in traffic is not recommended!

HILL CLIMBING—One of the oldest forms of competition is racing against the clock up a steep slope. The most famous hill climb is just outside Muskegon, Michigan, at a sand dune known as Mt. Garfield. The course is 320 feet long with the finish line 20 feet below the crest of the hill. The Muskegon Hill Climb has been shown on national television, and its repute is such that 306 concrete steps alongside the course leading to the top have been donated by motorcycle clubs in thirty-six states, Canada and England.

SPEED WEEK—Late every August are the Bonneville Speed Trials, which are open to motorcyclists as well as automobile hot rodders. The runs are over a measured mile course.

PROFESSIONAL COMPETITION

SHORT TRACK RACING—Racing is on the oval, which is less than a half mile in length. Tracks may have a slight banking in the turns, but generally they are flat, hence the common term "flat tracking." Bikes are 250cc in engine size.

SPEEDWAY RACING—A specialized form of short track racing is notable for its fuel-burning 500cc bikes, which have rigid frames, and for its peculiar riding technique. Riders lean their bikes over in the turns but actually stand up to provide better traction while they fly through the corners without much backing off on the throttle. Tracks are dirt, usually less than a quarter-mile in length, although some speedway racing is done on tracks up to one-half mile around. Races are usually only four laps apiece.

HALF-MILE AND MILE RACING—Turns are usually flat, and speeds are faster. Novices continue to race 250cc machines, but juniors and experts use 750cc bikes which hit speeds of 115 to 120 mph on the mile tracks. Mile tracks are usually reserved for AMA national championship events and are either horse racing tracks or county fairgrounds used regularly for horse and auto racing.

TT STEEPLECHASE—A dirt race over a very tight, unpaved but graded and packed road course that includes one jump. It is normally one-half to two miles in length.

ROAD RACING—Motorcycles can race on any paved road course or even public roads used by automobiles. Tracks usually range in length from 1.5 to 4 miles with as many as 20 turns, although the famed course on the Isle of Man is 37.75 miles and has more than 200 corners.

DESERT RACING—Special events, such as the Mint 400 in Nevada and Baja 500 in Mexico, are held on closed courses over rugged country. The Nevada race is eight laps around a roughly 50-mile course, and the Baja 500 is one loop of about 500 miles. The Baja 1000—like the San Diego-to-Phoenix races half a century ago—goes from point to point. It starts in Ensenada, about 60 miles south of the American border in Baja California, and ends in La Paz near the tip of the Mexican peninsula 836 miles away.

DRAG RACING—While some of it involves racing for trophies, very little drag racing is available to the motorcyclist and is usually promoted by drag strips on a professional basis to draw the top names. Drag racing is simply an acceleration contest on pavement matching two riders over a quarter-mile course. In some areas the course is only 1000 yards or even as short as one-eighth mile.

OTHER EVENTS—Some of the previously mentioned types of racing described as amateur are also promoted on a professional basis, such as motocross and hill climbing.

HOW TO GET INTO RACING

The major racing organization in the United States is the American Motorcycle Association, which sanctions nearly 7000 motorcycle races a year, including 500 professional events. Through the AMA 60,000 riders compete in a year, most of them in amateur racing events staged by 2000 local clubs chartered by the AMA. The association has a membership of 130,000, which makes it the largest racing organization in the world.

Once a rider ventures beyond local club racing into the professional category, he is classed as a novice. He must compete as a novice for at least one year, but he will remain a novice at least until he earns the minimum number of points awarded for his racing performances. Next the racer becomes a junior rider. He remains in that class at least a year and until he earns additional points to achieve expert status. Experts can campaign nationally on the premiere circuit of the country, the AMA Grand National series of dirt track, TT steeplechase and road racing events, in quest of the championship. The epitome in American racing is to win the Number 1 plate that is assigned to the champion each year.

To apply for a racing license the beginning rider must be eighteen years of age and must join the American Motorcycle Association. Information is available by writing to the AMA at 5655 North High Street, Worthington, Ohio 43085.

There are other sanctioning organizations, whose racing activities are regularly publicized by the weekly motorcycle newspapers, which are available on newsstands and at some tracks. The two most important are *Cycle News* and *Motorcycle Weekly*. Most motorcycle dealerships are club and racing minded, and can usually put the aspiring racer in touch with local organizations which stage racing events.

8

Flagpole Sitting on a Bike

It was twenty minutes to nine. The sun was rising steadily in the sky over the oven-like Mojave Desert when Don Woods coasted into the agricultural inspection station west of Needles, California.

"I can't go on," he said. "It'll take me all day to cross this desert, and I can't see."

Don Woods abandoned his project to set a coast-to-coast record for riding a 125cc motorcycle. In less than four days he had guided a Harley-Davidson Rapido from Maine to California at speeds up to 60 mph. He was short of his goal, which was to start with the rear wheel in the Atlantic Ocean and end with the front wheel in the Pacific. Still, his performance was impressive.

With little more machine preparation than to install a bigger fuel tank and change the handlebars, Woods rode from Maine to California in 3 days 17 hours 25 minutes. He made a simple carburetor repair in New York, rode through sheets of rain in Missouri and Oklahoma, lost his lights and received a traffic citation in Arizona and nearly collapsed from exhaustion when he sighted the California border. The bike was capable of going on, but the rider had had it.

Why do motorcyclists do crazy things like that? Many of them must have a little Cannonball Baker in their blood.

Erwin G. Baker was born near Lawrenceburg, Indiana, on March 12, 1882. His father was a railroad man in Indianapolis, and young

140

Erwin became an apprentice machinist earning 88¢ a day. He worked out every night in a gymnasium and became an accomplished tumbler. While touring with an acrobatic team he developed an act where he punched five bags at once, with his fists, feet and head. Soon he graduated to vaudeville, where he worked for $100 a week, but in 1906 he got homesick in San Francisco and quit the show. A few hours after he had left town, the hotel where Baker had been staying collapsed during the historic San Francisco earthquake.

Back to work in Indianapolis, Baker bought a motorcycle, which he decided to try racing during a Fourth of July celebration in Crawfordsville, Indiana, in 1908. He won his first race and finished second in the next one, and that decided his future career. He practiced going around corners at full speed for a year and then turned professional.

Many motor racing fans know that the first Indianapolis 500 was held in 1911, but not many realize that the first race at Indianapolis Motor Speedway was a combined motorcycle and auto race event in 1909. During the three-day meeting Baker won the 10-mile national championship race. George Hendee of Indian sent him on a 14,000-mile good will tour of Cuba, Jamaica and Panama to help open those countries to motorcycle sales.

After that Baker became known as a "transcontinentalist." He earned the nickname "Cannonball" after he crossed the finish line of his first important run, San Diego to New York on a motorcycle in 1914, after 11 days 12 hours 10 minutes. Because he roared across the finish line so fast an unknown New York City newspaperman wrote that he "came like a cannonball," and the name stuck.

Baker had never ridden the bike he used until three hours before he began the run. To get to New York he crossed four mountain ranges, 1027 miles of desert, 232 miles of prairie mud and 64 miles down a railroad track. The route took him from 200 feet below sea level at Salton Sea to 10,000 feet up in the Rockies. He covered a total of 3378.9 miles.

It must be remembered that roads in that period were little better than cow paths. But Cannonball Baker was more than an ordinary motorcyclist. In 1916 he went to Australia to set a 24-hour endurance record. Through torrential rain, despite dodging rabbits and parakeets, he covered 1018.75 miles and set records at 200, 300 and 1000 miles. One night on the board track at Cincinnati he was trying for a 24-hour record when he took off his goggles. A bug hit him in the eye so hard he was knocked off the machine. Cannonball got back on and kept going to reach 1534.75 miles within the time allotted. Once in Indiana he was thrown off his bike when he hit a fence and was flipped onto the back of a grazing cow.

In 1917 Alan Bedell broke Baker's cross-country record with a transcontinental run in 7 days 16 hours 16 minutes. That was all the excuse Baker needed to make another run. Up to that point, counting runs he had made in automobiles, he had been across the country thirty-eight times.

Baker started in New York City June 19, 1919, crossing by ferry to Perth Amboy, New Jersey. In little more than two hours he was in Philadelphia dodging Sunday drivers. Riding through the Laurel Mountains of Pennsylvania he hit thunderstorms, but he was managing to keep ahead of the record. In less than twenty-four hours he was in Terre Haute, Indiana, where he stopped to sleep. The run came to naught, however, as Baker was arrested in Illinois the next day while trying to ride down a railroad track.

In 1921 Baker started a transcontinental run in a sidecar. He had a rider who was supposed to be relieved halfway across the country in Marshall, a small town in Missouri. Baker and his passenger arrived on schedule, but the relief rider was nowhere in sight. They canvassed all the hotels and finally found him in the local jail. Police had figured he was a nut because he talked of waiting there for someone to pick him up on a motorcycle.

On September 23, 1922, Baker started in Los Angeles bound for New York City, where he arrived on September 28th after 6 days 22 hours 52 minutes of solo riding. His speeds had ranged from 75 mph on the good roads—which were improving in those years—to 6 mph on desert sand.

In 1941, at the age of fifty-nine, he made his last coast-to-coast run on a motorcycle in 6 days and 7 hours. Baker died at the age of seventy-eight in Indianapolis.

Baker's record was surpassed by John Penton in 1959, and it stood at 52 hours 11 minutes when a Hungarian-born student, who

The end of the line for a hill climber, who falls backward on a wind-swept knoll as spectators watch.

fled to this country after the 1956 insurrection, decided he would try to make the run in less than forty-eight hours in 1968.

Tibor Sarossy of Fairview Park, Ohio, received a lot of encouragement from Penton, who had a shop near his home and had sold Sarossy his first motorcycle. Taking his own street bike, a BMW R69S that had 22,000 miles behind it, Sarossy clocked in at the Western Union Office in New York at midnight one day and at the Western Union office in Los Angeles 45 hours and 41 minutes later.

Sarossy's record run was more a nightmare than a race against the clock. Before he reached the Lincoln Tunnel he got lost because the road to the turnpike had been closed to traffic. Patches of heavy fog slowed him in West Virginia. In Oklahoma, rain awaited Sarossy as the sun went down. He began making stops, drinking black coffee and gulping down vitamin pills, hoping the time that passed would bring him closer to the end of the rainstorm. Near Amarillo, Texas, the rain was complicated by heavy winds. Near the New Mexico border the rain lightened, the wind grew stronger and there were streaks of lightning in the western skies ahead. Beyond Tucumcari, New Mexico, were rain, hail, lightning and flooded conditions. Sarossi stopped at a gas station, almost convinced he should not go farther. He was wet, cold, frightened and discouraged. At the gas station he asked if the rain was expected to stop, and an old Indian said, "Within ten miles, my son, you will be out of it."

He was, but the worst part of the run still was ahead of him, the Arizona-California desert. Filling up with fuel in Flagstaff, Arizona, he plunged into it. At the California agricultural inspection station Sarossy made his last stop, and it might have ended the run.

Parking the motorcycle, he felt the blood drain from his face and told the inspector, "I am going to faint," then he fell in the door of the station. Sarossy came to three minutes later, was given salt pills and water and continued to the Western Union office in downtown Los Angeles. Sarossy had averaged 58.7 mph while covering 2687 miles.

Another cross-country record run was originated in 1915 by Cannonball Baker, who rode from Vancouver, British Columbia, to Tijuana, Mexico, a distance of 1835.5 miles, in 3 days 9 hours 15 minutes. This was the first endurance test to be known as the "Three Flags Run." In 1936 Fred Ham of Pasadena, California, lowered the time from the Canadian to the Mexican border to 28 hours 7 minutes. In 1960 two Los Angeles policemen, Roxy Rockwood and Doug Woodward, teamed to lower the record to 16 hours 35 minutes, although by this time the distance had been shortened to 1480 miles of vastly improved highways. Woodward knocked that time down in 1961 with a solo run in 25 hours. In 1969 Darrell Triber of Spokane, Washington, became the first man to cover the distance in less than 24 hours with a time of 23 hours 35 minutes. On May 14, 1971 a 38-year-old truck driver from Grants Pass, Oregon, W. E. (Boon) Bundock, rolled across the Mexican border in 23 hours exactly. He was ticketed once for hitting 75 mph near Fresno, California, but otherwise had an uneventful trip.

There is something magical about the Baja, California, peninsula, something that attracts the adventurous American to its rugged coastline, dusty deserts, green mountain valleys and quiet farming settlements, where the Gringo is greeted with few words of English but much graciousness. So close to civilization, to bedroom communities where TV aerials are an accepted part of the landscape, to smog and the rush to get ahead that traps city dwellers in their own ambitions, Baja is one of the most primitive places in the Western Hemisphere. Its people are unhurried, its scenery breathtaking and its remoteness relaxing.

This will change all too soon. President Echeverria of Mexico is opening the peninsula to the American tourist by improving the road between Ensenada and La Paz, laughingly called Mexican Highway 1. To the true "Baja buff" this is a shame. It means there will soon be resort hotels and Sunday traffic on the road. It means the end to an unspoiled part of the world that was so close and accessible to the man who wanted to "get away from it all."

Meanwhile, the very difficulty of the road to La Paz has presented a special challenge to the off-road motorcyclist. The same siren call of Baja that lures American outdoorsmen to the Mexican peninsula has been even more irresistible to the desert rider. For years the Baja run was something a few intrepid motorcyclists would attempt, but in 1962 two Californians, Dave Ekins and Bill Robertson, Jr., tried a timed excursion on a pair of Honda 250s. Ekins made the nearly 1000-mile run in 39 hours 54 minutes, Robertson less than an hour slower. Gasoline had to be dropped along the way to aid the two riders, but otherwise they were on their own.

In 1966 four men tried it on a pair of Triumph 500s and two 650s—Dave Ekins again, his famous desert racing brother Bud, Cliff Coleman and Eddie Mulder, all professional riders. They got lost in the fog once and ran out of gasoline another time (they had to wake up the driver of a gasoline truck to get refilled). Arriving in La Paz, they lost 10 minutes finding the Western Union office where they had planned to clock in, because the office had been moved. They still set a new record of 39 hours 46 minutes.

A solo rider, Kim Kimball, was next to succeed. He made his run during the Baja 1000 in November 1970. Starting in Tijuana, he crossed the starting line of the actual race sixty miles south of Ensenada after all the bikes and cars competing had already been flagged off. His idea was that if he needed assistance there were race officials and emergency crews all the way down the course to aid him. He made La Paz in 38 hours 54 minutes.

The most daring solo ride was accomplished by Doug Douglas, a thirty-seven-year-old motorcycle dealer from San Bernardino, California. Riding a Norton AJS 250 Stormer with an airplane and crew hopping down the peninsula to supply him with fuel and repairs if necessary, Douglas slashed 11 hours off the elapsed time. He made it in 27 hours 15 minutes on December 14, 1970. His only difficulties were getting his wheels caught in separate wheel ruts, causing him to fall just south of the halfway point. Soon after that he encountered a truck, left the "road" to pass it and encountered a rock at 50 mph. His crew changed his plugs and points for him once during the run. Since the final leg of the trip was made in darkness, he was on his own and would have no help should he need it.

Whether the runs are timed or merely logged on the odometer, long distance riding has a fascination for many intrepid men and women. The open road is mighty tempting.

William Hoge of Yakima, Washington, dreamed of making a cross-country motorcycle trip all during the time he was serving his country in World War II. In 1947 he was mustered out and splurged his severance pay on a motorbike, which he rode for 7600 miles across the country and back.

A. F. Muffley, age sixty-three, and his sixty-two-year-old wife in 1949 rode together on a motorcycle from their home in Galesburg,

World champion Joel Robert of Belgium in action.

Illinois, to McCook, Nebraska, three states away, to attend their granddaughter's wedding.

Two men pioneered the Alcan Highway in 1939 when they rode a pair of motorcycles from Fairbanks, Alaska, to Vancouver, British Columbia, in six months. Once they nearly died from eating poisonous water lilies. Another time they were saved from starvation by Indians who fed them caribou steaks. Then they went for six days with only a porcupine for food. Most of the 2250 miles they covered were over mountains where not even a trail existed. Charles C. Williams, a fifty-eight-year-old sourdough, and twenty-five-year-old John Logan, a hardware salesman, claimed they had proved it was possible to cut a highway through to Alaska. This was thought to be a rather dubious idea at the time.

On September 8, 1954, Dick Hutchins, Walter Rolfe, Lloyd McComb and Vern Hendrick made it to the summit of 14,242-foot White Mountain near Bishop, California, with a motorcycle, which had to be pushed most of the last 1200 feet. Their request to climb nearby Mt. Whitney, highest mountain in the Sierras, was denied by the U.S. Forest Service.

Malcolm Bottomley, an Argentinian of British descent, completed a 10,000-mile trip from Montreal to Buenos Aires on October 3, 1948. It took him seven months, and he had to detour once for several hundred miles to avoid a revolution. He passed through twelve countries and arrived in Buenos Aires wearing the British paratrooper uniform he had worn in World War II.

Spelling each other as their motorcycle circled the Montlhery Autodrome near Paris, George Monneret and his two sons, Jean and Pierre, set a non-stop endurance record of 40,076 kilometers —about 25,000 miles—in 24 days 21 hours 43 minutes 40 seconds, averaging 43 mph. It would have been faster, except Jean crashed and went to the hospital with several broken bones, and the run had to be delayed 20 hours. Actual running time was 21 days 9 hours 14 minutes 58 seconds because stops consumed the rest of the time.

Even before Cannonball Baker thought of riding a motorcycle from coast to coast, William P. Streiff rode a one-cyclinder bike from San Francisco to New York in 28 days in 1910.

The ultimate trip, tried by many but apparently completed by only one, ended on November 11, 1968, for Ike Taylor of San

Diego, California. He rode around the world on a motorcycle, a distance of 45,000 miles, of which he recorded 28,223 on the odometer of his Triumph Trophy 650. He used 520 gallons of gasoline, eighty-three quarts of oil, three chains, four sets of spark plugs, three sets of ignition contact points, several light bulbs, three air filters but only one set of tires. He timed his journey to catch summer on both sides of the Equator. Taylor started by touring Western Europe in July and August, spent September along the Mediterranean, October crossing Asia, where he encountered ice in the high mountain passes of Turkey and Afghanistan, India and Nepal in November, then on to Thailand and Maylasia, where he was caught by the beginning of the monsoon season near Singapore. He took a passenger ship to Perth, Australia, and rode the 3000 lonely miles across the barren desert to the east coast in February. From Sydney he caught another ship to Panama, when he disembarked to ride his motorcycle through Central America and Mexico en route to New York. The trip took almost one year to the day to complete.

Motorcycling has its humorous and poignant moments as well.

In Gavle, Sweden, Miss Irene Karkson borrowed a lightweight bike for a spin around the block. After she got on she realized she didn't know how to stop. So she rode it down the highway fifty miles until it ran out of gas. She took the train home.

Shortly before the bombing of Pearl Harbor, Dr. Eugene Kay announced that he had applied for a patent for the first combination motorcycle and flying machine. He called it a "Grasshopper." It would be designed to rise or descend vertically, fly at 120 mph and cruise along the highway at 60 per. Unfortunately, the Grasshopper never got off the ground.

By 1949 New Jersey State Police had been riding motorcycles for twenty-eight years. Officers heaved a sigh of relief when they checked the bulletin board on December 10th of that year. They had been given the order to park their bikes for the duration of the winter months because of the high injury rate on icy streets.

Douglas Chadwick went to jail for three months when he pleaded guilty to dangerous driving in Los Angeles. He admitted he rammed the motorcycle of Stanley E. Stevens when he saw his own girlfriend riding on the back.

Police in London put a stop to a deadly new game being played by motorcycle-riding Teddy Boys in 1959. In a café one member would put on a record, and they would all run out and jump on their bikes. The object was to ride one mile along the busy London motorway and then return to the restaurant before the record was over. The first one back got a free cup of tea.

In 1947 the archbishop of Paris issued an edict forbidding priests from riding motorcycles. He said the priests' cassocks were getting caught in the machines and causing accidents. Bicycles, he said, were okay.

Two seventeen-year-old boys were arrested in Copenhagen for stealing two organ pipes from a church to use for exhaust headers on their motorcycle.

John Miller of Los Angeles lost a traffic case in Alhambra Municipal Court, where he was charged with carrying an unsafe load on his motorcycle. Miller pleaded without success that his mongrel pooch, Baron von Red Dog, had ridden safely on the back of his bike for more than five years. Baron, part German shepherd and part chow, wore special goggles, a neck scarf and a black leather cap, rested his paws on Miller's back and barked at pedestrians. The California Highway Patrolman who stopped him thought Miller was endangering other motorists if not the dog, and the judge agreed. "That'll be fourteen dollars. Next case."

In 1969 a seventy-seven-year-old lady known as Grandma Ball was forced to give up her motorcycle operator's license in Southport, England, because she couldn't get insurance any more. "I can ride as well as any youngster," she protested.

At the age of ninety-five in 1953 George Dobson of Devizes, England, was given a three-year driver's license suspension because he had been riding his motorcycle recklessly and when the policeman arrested him a bottle of whiskey had fallen out of his coat pocket.

The police department in Cambridge, Maryland, got rid of its one and only motorcycle in 1952, because nobody on the force would ride it. Somebody got a bargain. It went for $152.

Lio and Berto, two professional soccer players in Manaus, Brazil, fought the first known gun duel on motorcycles. Charging at each other with guns blazing, they were cheered by spectators. The outcome wasn't very amusing, as Lio was wounded in the foot, thigh and back and crashed his motorcycle. Berto, not injured, hailed a passing motorist and made a getaway.

No examination of the motorcycle phenomenon would be complete without a study of Evel Knievel, who says, "I don't worry about the jumping so much, it's the landing that bothers me sometimes."

Bob Knievel has jumped his way into the hearts of people everywhere and into the hospital eleven times. His failures have made him as much of a legend as his successes. The least that can be said of him is that he is a shrewd promoter, and the most that he is a brave young man who has almost single-handedly upstaged the image of the Hells Angels and those Marlon Brando-ish movies about outlaw motorcycle gangs.

Evel's finest hour came one night in 1970 when he was jumping at the Cow Palace. The announcer read over the public address system a disparaging comment Knievel had made about the "Angels" in a *True Magazine* article, apparently not realizing the Hells Angels were in the audience that night. As Evel made his final approach to the jump, one of the outlaw motorcyclists hurled a tire iron at him. He missed.

"I'd have left it right there and ignored him," Knievel explained

Swedish moto-cross ace Sylvain Geboers takes a tricky downhill jump, the type of maneuver for which he is famous.

later, "but he jumped down out of the stands and made a menacing gesture at me. So I decked him."

That was a signal to other members of the gang, who leaped out of the stands and charged Knievel, by this time leaning on his cane. He got a little help from his friends as scores of spectators poured onto the floor of the arena, and fifteen members of the Hells Angels were hospitalized that night.

Evel Knievel began jumping with a motorcycle after he attended a Joie Chitwood automobile daredevil show in Montana. He also concentrated on ski jumping competition and won the Rocky Mountain championship three times to retire the trophy. Spurning an offer to become a professional ice hockey player, Knievel began racing Class C motorcycles while he perfected the jumping act. Typical of his subsequent record, he almost cleared one of his first jumps, over two mountain lions and a pen of fifty rattlesnakes. As he landed he knocked down the end of the rattlesnake cage, and the rattlers began slithering out onto the track. The crowd vanished.

The stuntman worked his act up to a standard thirteen cars, but for special shows he increased the length of the jump, not always successfully. At Caesar's Palace in Las Vegas, Nevada, he had his most famous miss when he jumped 150 feet, clearing the hotel's famous fountain. On landing, the motorcycle wobbled, and down went the cyclist—eventually to spend weeks in the hospital for multiple injuries. In true showman fashion, he conducted press conferences from his hospital bed and continued making arrangements for even bigger jumps. Turned down by the U.S. Department of Interior on his request for permission to jump one mile over an open space at the Grand Canyon, he acquired land along the Snake River in Idaho, where a jump was tentatively scheduled for July 1974, on a 300 mph water jet-powered bike, using super heated Olympia Beer for the jet propulsion medium.

The magic of Evel Knievel, the charisma that has charmed hundreds of thousands of spectators, is that he is a man who won't give up. Down many times but never out, he keeps returning for more hair-raising feats despite the possibility of terrible consequences. Once he told why he does his "thing":

"I was hospitalized and laid up for about six months," he said, recalling an early accident in his career. "I was not only broke physically, but I was broke financially. The only thing that wasn't broken was my outlook on the thing, and I wanted to get back up and keep doing it because it was a dream with me, and I really wanted to do it. And when you really want to to something bad enough, really want to do it, you can do it, no matter how bad you're hurt."

Evel Knievel has attracted a number of imitators, including one who claims the world record for a motorcycle jump. Gary Wells, age fourteen, jumped sixteen cars at an American Hot Rod Association meet (Evel has cleared twenty) but also cleared the receiving ramp on the other end of the jump. Landing on pavement, his front wheel collapsed, but he maintained control until the bike had slowed to 40 mph, when he fell off. Taking out his tape measure, AHRA President Jim Tice claimed a world record of 155 feet 10 inches and said it was sanctioned by Motorsports International, the new arm of AHRA which supervises non-drag racing events. The youngster, meanwhile, suffered only minor cuts and bruises and was able to sign 3000 autographs afterward.

Altogether there are about a half dozen leapers performing at motorcycle races, county fairs and sporting events around the country. But at this point in history, motorcycle enthusiasts will agree, there is only one Evel Knievel.

Another barn-stormer of today is a bespectacled young man named E. J. Potter, who tours drag strips with a Chevrolet-powered motorcycle. Using a Harley-Davidson 74 frame, which he split to insert the motor, he makes exhibition runs with the weird hybrid. He's even been in Australia.

Potter's favorite trick is to lean the bike over at 150 mph and zigzag down the track. His most harrowing experience came at a small track where he contracted to make three runs, and it started raining after his second one.

"The promoter didn't give out rain checks," Potter said, "and all the spectators went home. I told the guy that since he didn't give out rain checks, then I should get my full money. He said he'd pay, but that I would have to make another run. So I went out and made the final run on a wet track with only a handful of people watching. When I came back, he said, 'Boy, you sure lived up to your name—you are crazy.' I said it was his idea, not mine."

Somewhere on the county fair circuit you might run into a genuine wall rider. Those are fellows who ride a motorcycle around the rim of a wooden bowl 16 to 40 feet in diameter for the entertainment of carnival customers. Wall riders do fancy tricks, like standing up and going through acrobatic routines, and they occasionally fall. None of these routines, however, can match the "world record" high wire act done by a German acrobatic team on the cable between Sugar Loaf and Urca Mountains above Rio de Janeiro, Brazil, on June 16, 1951.

While Rudi Boehme held his motorcycle motionless on the cable used for the scenic cable car, his four partners hung a trapeze on the bike, and they did acrobatic stunts over a 600-foot chasm for an hour and a half.

The stunt riding that inflamed a nation, however, was performed by a mysterious Italian teen-ager, Antonio Mellini, who was dubbed "Agostini the Mad." One of nine children of a Neopolitan antique dealer, he appeared at midnight on August 23, 1970, without warning aboard his Ducati 125 to entertain the street people with a daring display of trick motorcycle riding. Leaping from chair to chair in sidewalk cafés, up and down the steps of public buildings, between strolling pedestrians terrifying them, he eluded police by vanishing into side streets. At midnight the following two nights he roared into town again and triggered a riot among the people who were clamoring to get a look at his trick riding. Police never were able to catch him.

Months later he was arrested while walking into a church and charged with "outraging public officials," an offense interpreted by the citizens of Naples as meaning he had made fools of the police, which he had. Public sentiment was so strong that when he came to trial in February 1971, the eighteen-year-old daredevil was given a suspended fourteen-month sentence. Meanwhile, he and his father pondered offers for him to appear in motion pictures and to have his autobiography ghostwritten. Italian sociologists called "Ago the Mad" a true folk hero, a symbol of youth who laughs at the pomposity of the establishment.

Someday, in this gimmicky world, a motorcyclist will lay claim to the world's longest wheelstand. We've personally witnessed Lee (Iron Man) Irons hold a wheelie for one mile down the pit lane at Ontario Motor Speedway, and no one who has seen him would doubt that he could hold one entirely around the 2.5-mile oval. Evel Knievel has said he could hold a wheelie indefinitely, given enough room to run.

There is also certain to be an official measurement of the best mileage ever achieved on a motorcycle. A distributor for a little known fold-up motorcycle called the Corgi claimed in 1948 that his machine—developed from the Welbike that was dropped to British paratroopers during World War II—had been tested at 140 miles per gallon. If that seems a little extravagant, there is probably a manufacturer right now figuring a way to beat it.

Anybody for flagpole sitting on a bike?

9
Two Wheels in Your Future

As far as motorcyclists are concerned, the year 1984 envisioned by George Orwell may get here sooner than expected. There seems to be little doubt that the government will take a more active part in control of the motorcycle by enforcing stricter safety, ecology, noise and consumer protection standards. The National Highway Traffic Safety Administration is already moving to influence licensing practices. Various government agencies at every level, from the cities to the federal government, are making it harder for motorcyclists to go where they want to go off the road. Laws concerning excessive noise are a direct result of the bike manufacturers not moving quickly enough to do something about making their products quieter. Noise laws also have been influenced by irresponsible riders who purposely have magnified their exhaust sounds with expansion chambers and megaphones that someday may be outlawed.

Eventually, legislators may even feel compelled to enact a law requiring all brake controls to be located on the right side of the motorcycle and all gear selectors on the left. There are still a few manufacturers which persist in reversing the normal setup, a condition consumer advocates like Ralph Nader find incomprehensible. Their heads are filled with visions of the rider making a panic stop, hitting what he thinks is the brake lever and shifting up into a higher gear instead. As we have all seen in recent years, government attitudes bend toward protecting the private citizen from his own folly.

New laws and their enforcement may take some of the fun out of motorcycling for its staunchest supporters, but there doesn't seem to be a limit to the expanding enthusiasm for the sport of motorcycle riding. No matter what happens to restrict enjoyment, there are apparently more and more people waiting in the wings to become interested in two-wheel recreation. The transition to a new era in motorcycle history has already taken place, in the words of Ivan Wagar, editor of *Cycle World*: "We don't have motorcyclists any more. We have people riding motorcycles."

The love of motorcycles no longer sets the enthusiast apart from others in society. The bike lover may once have been seen as a strange, eccentric, maybe even undesirable person who refuses to accept the realities of a four-wheel norm in this motorized world. "You meet the nicest people . . ." is an advertising slogan that literally made itself come true. Today's rider could just as easily be the boy or the girl next door. He or she is definitely no longer just a kook.

That the future of the motorcycle is directly tied to social conditions in which more time is becoming available for leisure and recreation cannot be argued against. We have of course seen it happen in America, where recreational motorcycling has boomed during a period of ever increasing affluence. People have more time on their hands and more money to spend. There are more younger people capable of buying the things they want, and younger people are more adventurous, on the go and seeking thrills, less inhibited, less interested in comformity, more healthy and able to engage in physical activities.

Soon most American wage earners will have a four-day week. Some already do. Psychologists, sociologists and urban planners are already worrying about what effect the new-found free time will have on the mental health of the four-day week employee. What to do with leisure will be one of the important questions of future generations. The sport of motorcycle riding may play an important role in that future.

There appears to be a definite pattern of interest in motorcycles, as seen in their popularity here and in Japan, for example.

Motorcycles competed with automobiles for acceptance as the best basic transportation in the early years of this century. The automobile, which offers more comfort and protection to the driver and his passengers, obviously won that competition. It wasn't until the Japanese manufacturers tried marketing the motorcycle as a recreation vehicle in the 1960s that sales figures zoomed upward in the United States. By contrast, Japan was selling motorcycles in its own country to people who needed basic transportation, and the marketing of transportation motorbikes was quite successful until the Japanese started making more money. Once they could afford automobiles, Japanese workers stopped buying motorcycles. Later, when Japanese manufacturers started selling to their own people bikes intended for export, they were pleasantly startled at the enthusiastic response. These were recreation machines.

There are many areas of the world where people need better transportation but can't afford the cost of an automobile or the expense of maintaining one. Into these countries several motorcycle

A modern motorcycle production line shows the combined features of automation and thorough individual inspection.

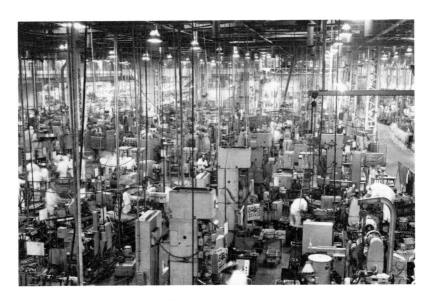

Another view of the Honda factory.

companies have gone with their products. It is too soon to tell, but it seems likely that two-wheel motor vehicles will become the rule in the lesser developed nations of the world in the next two decades, particularly in Southeast Asia and South America.

In highly developed societies, such as the one we have in the United States, it appears that traffic congestion may dictate a new transportation role for the motorcycle. One of the transport industry's more advanced thinkers, designer Alex Tremulis, sees a day when special lanes will be marked off on the freeways and expressways for motorcycles only. Lanes narrower than the ones where cars travel will allow faster transit for two-wheel commuters and remove much of the hazard of mixing automobiles and motorcycles from high speed travel. Tremulis goes further than that. He sees a design revolution ahead for the motorcycle industry.

The eccentric automobile stylist and designer who gave shape and advanced engineering ideas to the world's first safety car, the Tucker Torpedo, has long been associated with the idea that man can someday stabilize a two-wheel vehicle with a gyroscope to produce the ultimate in safety, maneuverability and speed in an automobile. Tremulis was even associated with a project to perfect a "gyro-mobile" at one time, but it got bogged down in experimentation and eventually ran out of money.

Tremulis' Gyronaut X-1 Bonneville streamliner ridden by Bob Leppan was the forerunner of a series of Land Speed Record two-wheelers intended to be based on gyrostabilization. Gyronaut X-2 was to be the first two-wheeler with a gyroscope aboard to overcome the difficulty of getting a heavy vehicle from 0 to 100 mph quickly and decelerating to a stop. It would have been powered by a popular engine of the day, the 289-cubic-inch Ford Cobra, and had a design speed of 400 mph. This same two-wheeler powered by a fuel-burning supercharged hemi Chrysler, typical of the engines found in fuel-burning dragsters and funny cars, had a potential of 500 mph, according to the designer. Finally, Tremulis was ready to plunge the gyrostabilized motorcycle into the unknown, beyond the speed of sound, with rocket power. Gyronaut X-3 was to weigh 3000 pounds, nearly half of which would consist of solid propellant. Firing three sets of rockets in sequence 5 seconds each for a total of 15 seconds at 9000 pounds thrust, the vehicle would be capable of covering a standing quarter-mile in 5.7 seconds and reaching 360 mph at the end of the quarter—or of streaking through the sound barrier and leaving it behind on the way to a maximum velocity near 1000 mph.

Due to the failure to date of anyone to produce a gyroscope system for a motor vehicle, none of this has happened. It is all in the mind of a somewhat practical dreamer, Tremulis. Why, you might ask, bother to go to Bonneville at all with such a radical two-wheeler?

The Gyronaut land record bikes were part of a grand scheme that could spearhead a revolution in the transportation sciences. The Bonneville runs were to demonstrate the efficiency of two-wheel transport for man. Single track vehicles offer many advantages over two-track automobiles. They are more narrow and thus have better aerodynamics and fuel economy. They can be made smaller, lighter, lower and longer (with gyrostabilization). They offer the stylist almost an unlimited range of shapes, whereas the four-wheel automobile is very restrictive to the designer.

Tremulis' imagination wandered over a new world of exciting challenge for the motorcycle builder. He foresaw trucks and buses on two wheels, army tanks, construction equipment, firefighting rigs that could travel almost vertically up steep mountain trails, lunar exploring cars, even commuter trains that could travel safely at speeds of more than 250 mph.

The one flaw in his plan was that the world still waits for someone to perfect a stabilizing gyro for an automobile. Once that is done, a safe vehicle must be guaranteed before the public will accept it. One of the more important questions left unanswered is: What happens to the gyroscope in a serious accident?

Returning to the practical world, which has no gyromobile, Tremulis still sees a new era approaching for the motorcycle industry, with exciting, radically different machines offered to enthusiasts in the near future.

"Look at the history of motorcycles," Tremulis said. "The motorcycle hasn't changed much since the beginning. It has had a very slow evolutionary development in comparison with the automobile. I believe the motorcycle is ready now for revolutionary change."

The motorcycle of the future, he predicted, is a three-wheeler with banking capabilities. Tremulis calls it a "poor man's gyrocycle."

The designer developed his concept around a curious-looking "dream car" first proposed and patented in 1927 by the French designer Gabriel Voisin. It was diamond-shaped with four wheels in three separate tracks. Like a motorcycle, it had two main wheels fore and aft, and two side wheels served to stabilize it. This design enables the stylist to make use of the most efficient aerodynamic shape, the needle-nose configuration, and it suggested that head-on collisions might be reduced to minor bumps as the colliding pointed vehicles bounced off each other's sides. It also introduced the banking capability with which motorcyclists are so familiar but which is unknown in automobiles.

"I sometimes wonder," Tremulis commented, "if the future will ever catch up with the past."

From the Voisin diamond-shaped car, Tremulis evolved his Trigano. *Trigano* is a Greek work meaning "three points." The dream car as depicted by Tremulis is long and low, with seats for both the driver and the passengers side by side. They sit in automobile type seats, rather than straddling a saddle. The most important feature of the Trigano is its banking ability, which Tremulis claims whould make it a super stable vehicle, the perfect compromise between two- and four-wheel transport.

The Trigano would have the desirable features of needle-nose styling for cleaner aerodynamics, improved crash protection and better fuel economy. It would have the ideal dircctional stability of a motorcycle, which is superior to any other class of motor vehicle in the world in maintaining a straight line. It would protect the passengers not only from the terrible G forces of head-on crash impact due to the pointed nose, but riders would be further shielded by an enclosing body. The unpleasantness (to many people) of the blast of air against the motorcyclist's body would be eliminated by the fully enclosed cockpit, and, of course, comfort would be greatly improved by bucket seats rather than the traditional saddle. Tremulis also claims that the elimination of placing the foot down to maintain stability at the parked position would be a great new plus factor for the three-wheel concept.

"A lot of people are hurt parking their motorcycles," he said. "Police especially have a significant injury rate caused by bikes falling on them."

In contrast to present three-wheel motorcycles and sidecars, Tremulis claimed the Trigano would be a very stable vehicle under a variety of conditions. The so-called dunecycle, he said, is "the most dangerous vehicle in the world today" based on its unusual center of gravity and top-heaviness.

The "poor man's gyrocycle" would have a wheelbase more of automotive than of motorcycle dimensions, something over 100 inches. The stretched wheelbases of Bonneville streamliners, Tremulis claimed, support his premise that the longer the wheelbase the more stable a two-wheeler is in a straight line, and he claims that a banking three-wheeler is subject to the same design superiority a motorcycle has over an automobile.

To develop his theories about motorcycles of the future into something practical for the street today, Tremulis did a small scale survey of several police departments in the vicinity of his Ventura, California, home. He found to his horror that motorcycle policemen averaged three trips to the hospital each year, and that in about one accident in four an officer could expect to suffer a serious injury. The three major causes of police accidents, according to Tremulis, were scrapes with automobiles, falling down and high speed wobble. While the benefits of motorcycle use by police are well documented, the hazards are also well known. Most officers will not ride in the rain or join in a chase at speeds over 80 mph (they'll radio ahead and try to set up roadblocks). A flat tire while out in the field often requires the services of a truck and a crew of three. Sirens operated by a rotor touching the front tire have a tendency to blow out the tire if they are started at more than 50 mph.

Tremulis's ideas on three-wheel bikes have been enthusiastically received by the police officials he has talked to. Whether or not motorcycle manufacturers will take seriously his proposals for a half-bike, half-auto like the Trigano remains for the future to be told. It seems clear, however, that motorcycles will become more civilized in the near future.

Industry observers make the following predictions:

(1) There will probably be retractable landing struts or wheels on motorbikes soon. They would be manually, electrically or vacuum operated, possibly triggered by an on-board computer which signals the "training wheels" to lower or raise themselves at certain speeds or while the bike is at a standstill. The landing gear approach to holding a bike up while stopped at a signal, while starting the machine or while parked would eliminate a good share of accidents and would permit motorcycles to be designed for more rider comfort. Keeping feet on the pegs or on a floorboard would be more than a comfort aid. It would give the rider more control.

(2) The sit-down seat will eventually replace the saddle. Purists who love motorcycles for the sheer enjoyment of having to manage them—wrestling them around and giving them commands like those a cowboy conveys to his horse with the heel of his boot —will probably object. But the more comfortable position offers many advantages. A comfortable rider is said to be better equipped to look out for his own safety. His machine is "idiot proofed."

(3) Stylists will change the bare bones appearance of today's motorcycles to futuristic, bullet-like enclosed machines that will sit very low to the ground. They will be popular low-price substitutes for sports cars.

(4) Eventually motorcycles will become as quiet as automobiles, perhaps even quieter, as the industry either takes leadership in eliminating its noise problem or responds to the prodding of the government.

(5) Three-wheelers with banking abilities as high as 40 degrees will become the fastest and safest machines on the street. Rocket powered versions could set Land Speed records approaching Mach 2 (about 1400 mph).

(6) Sophisticated running gear systems may eventually replace the traditional chain drive, just as the chain replaced the leather belt of early motorcycles. The three-wheeler will introduce such automotive niceties as the differential and the automatic transmission.

(7) Wheels may become smaller as design problems of setting the operator lower on his bike are overcome, and brakes will of course improve.

(8) Multi-passenger vehicles will be made possible by the introduction of "training wheels" or gyrostabilization or some method of maintaining the two-wheel vehicle in an upright position when it is not in motion. Two-wheel trucks, buses and trains are not flights of fancy. They could be easily built using today's technology. The problem remains: Who would buy them?

(9) Off-road riding will become more civilized, following a trend observed by knowledgeable people like Wagar. In the northeastern United States, where cyclists are in the habit of riding woods and trail bikes and do not have a craze for speed, there are hundreds of miles of trails for them to use. They get along nicely with equestrians and hikers too. This is no accident. It resulted from a campaign spearheaded by Bob Hicks, publisher of *Cycle Sport*, and others. In the West, however, the noise, litter, destruction and other side effects of uncontrolled off-road riding have taken their toll. It is almost too late for motorcyclists to negotiate for the use of riding space. The commercial motorcycle park takes care of some but not all of the demand. Motorcyclists will have to

A lone rider pauses to survey some of the wide trails provided at a typical motorcycle recreation park in Southern California, where off-road riding has become severely restricted by authorities.

become more responsible and motorcycles more acceptable to the public at large or off-road riding will disappear.

(10) There will always be a motorcycle as we know it today. As long as there are free thinking, exploration-oriented men and women who enjoy the feel of wind against their bodies and enjoy mastery of a machine as personal as a motorcycle, there will be manufacturers willing to provide them. The motorbike does not seem destined to go the way of the horse and buggy.

10 Charts

early unofficial motorcycle records

Location and Date	Mph	Rider, Country	Cycle
(1) **1903**	60	Unknown	British Excelsior
(2) **1904**	67.4	Glenn Curtiss, USA	Curtiss
(2) **1907**	136.364	Glenn Curtiss, USA	Curtiss V8 prototype
1908	68	Liese, Germany	NSU Twin
1909	77.06	Otto Lingenfelder, Germany	NSU-LA
1910	94.92	Charlie Collier, England	Matchless V Twin

recognized motorcycle land speed records

(2) **Apr. 14, 1920**	103.77	Eugene Walker, USA	Indian OHV 61 1000cc
(3) **Nov. 6, 1923**	108.75	Claude Temple, England	BR-Anzani V Twin 1000cc
(4) **July 6, 1924**	119.31	Bert LeVack, England	Brough Superior JAP 1000cc
(4) **Sept. 5, 1926**	121.42	Claude Temple, England	Temple V Twin 1000cc
(2) **1926**	*132.001	Johnny Seymour, USA	Indian 611N
(4) **Aug. 25, 1928**	124.90	Baldwin, England	Zenith JAP 1000cc
(4) **Aug. 25, 1929**	129.25	Bert LeVack, England	Brough Superior 1000cc

Location and Date	Mph	Rider, Country	Cycle
(5) **Sept. 19, 1929**	134.757	Ernst Henne, Germany	BMW 750cc
(4) **Aug. 31, 1930**	137.320	J.S. Wright, England	Temple JAP 1000cc
(5) **Sept. 21, 1930**	137.354	Ernst Henne, Germany	BMW 750cc
(6) **Nov. 6, 1930**	150.736	J.S. Wright, England	Temple JAP 1000cc (first streamliner)
(7) **Nov. 2, 1932**	151.760	Ernst Henne, Germany	BMW 750cc
(7) **Oct. 30, 1934**	152.900	Ernst Henne, Germany	BMW 750cc
(8) **Sept. 27, 1935**	159.100	Ernst Henne, Germany	BMW 750cc
(8) **Oct. 12, 1936**	168.912	Ernst Henne, Germany	BMW 750cc
(2) **Mar. 13, 1937**	*136.183	Joe Petrali, USA	Harley-Davidson
(7) **Apr. 19, 1937**	169.786	Eric Fernihough, England	Brough Superior JAP 1000cc
(9) **Oct. 21, 1937**	170.260	Piero Taruffi, Italy	Gilera-Rondine 500cc
(8) **Nov. 28, 1937**	173.880	Ernst Henne, Germany	BMW 500cc
(12) **1950**	*156.71	Roland Free, USA	Harley-Davidson
(10) **Apr. 12, 1951**	180.090	Wilhelm Herz, Germany	NSU 500cc
(11) **July 2, 1955**	185.058	Russell Wright, New Zealand	Vincent HRD 1000cc
(12) **Aug. 4, 1956**	210.640	Wilhelm Herz, Germany	NSU 500cc
(12) **Sept. 6, 1956**	214.400	Johnny Allen, USA	Triumph 650cc
(12) **Aug. 28, 1958**	214.470	Jess Thomas, USA	Triumph 650cc
(12) **Aug. 24, 1962**	230.269	Bill Johnson, USA	Triumph 650cc
(12) **Aug. 25, 1966**	245.667	Bob Leppan, USA	Gyronaut X-1 Triumph (two 650s) 1300cc
(12) **Sept. 17, 1970**	251.924	Don Vesco, USA	Yamaha 350cc
(12) **Oct. 16, 1970**	265.492	Cal Rayborn, USA	Harley-Davidson Stroker 3000cc

*—Not officially recognized by the FIM.

Locations for Record Runs—(1) Dublin, Ireland. (2) Daytona Beach, Florida. (3) Brooklands race track, England. (4) Arpajon, France. (5) Schleifheim Autobahn, Germany. (6) Cork, Ireland. (7) Gyon-Bud Road, Hungary. (8) Frankfurt Autobahn, Germany. (9) Bergamo, Italy. (10) Munich Autobahn, Germany. (11) Swannonoa, New Zealand. (12) Bonneville Salt Flats, Wendover, Utah.

The Isle of Man Tourist Trophy champions

Year	Race Class	Miles	Rider	Make	Mph
1907	Twins	158⅛	H. Remington Fowler	Norton	36.22
	Singles	158⅛	Charlie R. Collier	Matchless	38.22
1908	Twins	158⅛	Harry Reed	DOT	38.59
	Singles	158⅛	Jack Marshall	Triumph	40.49

Year	Race Class	Miles	Rider	Make	Mph
1909		158⅛	Harry A. Collier	Matchless	49.01
1910		158⅛	Charlie R. Collier	Matchless	50.63
1911	Senior	187½	O. C. Godfrey	Indian	47.63
	Junior	150	P. J. Evans	Humber	41.45
1912	Senior	187½	Frank Applebee	Scott	48.69
	Junior	150	Harry Bashall	Douglas	39.65
1913	Senior	262½	H. O. (Tim) Wood	Scott	48.27
	Junior	225	Hugh Mason	NUT	43.75
1914	Senior	225	Cyril G. Pullin	Rudge	49.49
	Junior	187½	Eric Williams	AJS	45.58
1920	Senior	226½	Tommy de la Hay	Sunbeam	51.48
	Junior 350cc	187½	Cyril Williams	AJS	40.74
	Junior 250cc	187½	R. O. Clark	Levis	38.30
1921	Senior	226½	Howard Davies	350cc AJS	54.50
	Junior 350cc	187½	Eric Williams	AJS	52.11
	Junior 250cc	187½	D. G. Prentice	New Imperial	44.61
1922	Senior	226½	Alec Bennett	Sunbeam	58.31
	Junior	187½	Tom Sheard	AJS	54.75
	Lightweight	187½	Geoff S. Davison	Levis	49.89
1923	Senior	226½	Tom Sheard	Douglas	55.55
	Junior	226½	Stanley Woods	Cotton	55.73
	Lightweight	226½	Jock Porter	New Gerrard	51.93
	Sidecar	113¼	Fred Dixon	Douglas	53.15
1924	Senior	226½	Alec Bennett	Norton	61.64
	Junior	226½	Kenneth Twemlow	New Imperial	55.67
	Lightweight	226½	Eddie Twemlow	New Imperial	55.44
	Ultra-Lightweight	113¼	Jock Porter	New Gerrard	51.20
	Sidecar	151	G. H. Tucker	Norton	51.31
1925	Senior	226½	Howard R. Davies	HRD	66.13
	Junior	226½	Wal Handley	Rex-Acme	65.02
	Lightweight	226½	Eddie Twemlow	New Imperial	57.74
	Ultra-Lightweight	151	Wal Handley	Rex-Acme	53.45
	Sidecar	151	L. Parker	Douglas	55.22
1926	Senior	264¼	Stanley Woods	Norton	67.54
	Junior	264¼	Alec Bennett	Velocette	66.70

Year	Race Class	Miles	Rider	Make	Mph
	Lightweight	264¼	C. W. (Paddy) Johnston	Cotton	60.20
1927	Senior	264¼	Alec Bennett	Norton	68.41
	Junior	264¼	Freddie Dixon	HRD	67.19
	Lightweight	264¼	Wal Handley	Rex-Acme	63.30
1928	Senior	264¼	Charlie J. P. Dodson	Sunbeam	62.98
	Junior	264¼	Alec Bennett	Velocette	68.65
	Lightweight	264¼	Frank Longman	O.K. Supreme	62.90
1929	Senior	264¼	Charlie J. P. Dodson	Sunbeam	72.05
	Junior	264¼	F. G. Hicks	Velocette	69.71
	Lightweight	264¼	Syd Crabtree	Excelsior	63.87
1930	Senior	264¼	Wal Handley	Rudge	74.24
	Junior	264¼	H. G. Tyrell-Smith	Rudge	71.08
	Lightweight	264¼	A. James Guthrie	AJS	64.71
1931	Senior	264¼	P. (Tim) Hunt	Norton	77.90
	Junior	264¼	P. (Tim) Hunt	Norton	73.94
	Lightweight	264¼	Graham W. Walker	Rudge	68.98
1932	Senior	264¼	Stanley Woods	Norton	79.38
	Junior	264¼	Stanley Woods	Norton	77.16
	Lightweight	264¼	Leo H. Davenport	New Imperial	70.48
1933	Senior	264¼	Stanley Woods	Norton	81.04
	Junior	264¼	Stanley Woods	Norton	78.08
	Lightweight	264¼	S. Gleave	Excelsior	71.59
1934	Senior	264¼	A. James Guthrie	Norton	78.01
	Junior	264¼	A. James Guthrie	Norton	79.16
	Lightweight	264¼	Jimmy H. Simpson	Rudge	70.81
1935	Senior	264¼	Stanley Woods	Moto Guzzi	84.68
	Junior	264¼	A. James Guthrie	Norton	79.14
	Lightweight	264¼	Stanley Woods	Moto Guzzi	71.56
1936	Senior	264¼	A. James Guthrie	Norton	85.80
	Junior	264¼	Freddie L. Frith	Norton	80.14
	Lightweight	264¼	A. R. (Bob) Foster	New Imperial	74.28
1937	Senior	264¼	Freddie L. Frith	Norton	88.21
	Junior	264¼	A. James Guthrie	Norton	84.43
	Lightweight	264¼	Omobono Tenni	Guzzi	74.72
1938	Senior	264¼	Harold L. Daniell	Norton	89.11
	Junior	264¼	Stanley Woods	Velocette	84.08
	Lightweight	264¼	Ewald Kluge	DKW	78.48
1939	Senior	264¼	Georg Meier	BMW	89.38
	Junior	264¼	Stanley Woods	Velocette	83.19
	Lightweight	264¼	E. A. Mellors	Benelli	74.25

Year	Race Class	Miles	Rider	Make	Mph
1947	Senior	264¼	Harold L. Daniell	Norton	82.81
	Junior	264¼	Bob Foster	Velocette	80.31
	Lightweight	264¼	Manliff Barrington	Guzzi	73.22
1948	Senior	264¼	Artie J. Bell	Norton	84.97
	Junior	264¼	Freddie L. Frith	Velocette	81.45
	Lightweight	264¼	Maurice Cann	Guzzi	75.18
1949	Senior	264¼	Harold L. Daniell	Norton	86.93
	Junior	264¼	Freddie L. Frith	Velocette	83.15
	Lightweight	264¼	Manliff Barrington	Guzzi	77.96
1950	Senior	264¼	Geoff E. Duke	Norton	92.27
	Junior	264¼	Artie J. Bell	Norton	86.33
	Lightweight	264¼	Dario Ambrosini	Benelli	78.08
1951	Senior	264¼	Geoff E. Duke	Norton	93.83
	Junior	264¼	Geoff E. Duke	Norton	89.90
	Lightweight 250cc	151	Tommy L. Wood	Guzzi	81.39
	Lightweight 125cc	75½	Cromie McCandless	Mondial	74.85
1952	Senior	264¼	H. Reg Armstrong	Norton	92.97
	Junior	264¼	Geoff E. Duke	Norton	90.29
	Lightweight 250cc	151	Fergus K. Anderson	Guzzi	83.82
	Lightweight 125cc	113¼	Cecil C. Sandford	MV	75.54
1953	Senior	264¼	W. Ray Amm	Norton	93.85
	Junior	264¼	W. Ray Amm	Norton	90.52
	Lightweight 250cc	151	Fergus K. Anderson	Guzzi	84.73
	Lightweight 125cc	113¼	Les Graham	MV	77.79
1954	Senior	151	W. Ray Amm	Norton	88.12
	Junior	188¾	Rod Coleman	AJS	91.51
	Lightweight 250cc	113¼	Werner Haas	NSU	90.88
	Lightweight 125cc	114	Rupert Hollaus	NSU	69.57
	Sidecar	114	Eric Oliver	Norton	68.87
1955	Senior	264¼	Geoff E. Duke	Gilera	97.93
	Junior	264¼	Bill Lomas	Guzzi	92.33
	Lightweight 250cc	97	Bill Lomas	MV	71.37
	Lightweight 125cc	97	Carlo Ubbiali	MV	69.67

Year	Race Class	Miles	Rider	Make	Mph
	Sidecar	97	Willy Schneider	BMW	70.01
1956	Senior	264¼	John Surtees	MV	96.57
	Junior	264¼	Ken T. Kavanagh	Guzzi	89.29
	Lightweight 250cc	97	Carlo Ubbiali	MV	67.05
	Lightweight 125cc	97	Carlo Ubbiali	MV	69.13
	Sidecar	97	Fritz Hillebrand	BMW	70.03
1957	Senior	302	Bob McIntyre	Gilera	98.99
	Junior	264¼	Bob McIntyre	Gilera	94.99
	Lightweight 250cc	107½	Cecil C. Sandford	Mondial	75.80
	Lightweight 125cc	107½	Tarquinio Provini	Mondial	73.69
	Sidecar	107½	Fritz Hillebrand	BMW	71.89
1958	Senior	264¼	John Surtees	MV	98.63
	Junior	264¼	John Surtees	MV	93.97
	Lightweight 250cc	107½	Tarquinio Provini	MV	76.89
	Lightweight 125cc	107½	Carlo Ubbiali	MV	72.86
	Sidecar	107½	Willy Schneider	BMW	73.01
1959	Senior	264¼	John Surtees	MV	87.94
	Junior	264¼	John Surtees	MV	95.38
	Lightweight 250cc	107½	Tarquinio Provini	MV	77.77
	Lightweight 125cc	107½	Tarquinio Provini	MV	74.06
	Sidecar	107½	Willy Schneider	BMW	72.69
	Formula 1 500cc	113¼	Bob McIntyre	Norton	97.77
	Formula 1 350cc	113¼	Alistair King	AJS	94.66
1960	Senior	226½	John Surtees	MV	102.44
	Junior	226½	John Hartle	MV	96.70
	Lightweight 250cc	188¾	Gary Hocking	MV	93.64
	Lightweight 125cc	113¼	Carlo Ubbiali	MV	85.60
	Sidecar	113¼	Helmut Fath	BMW	84.10
1961	Senior	226½	Mike Hailwood	Norton	100.60
	Junior	226½	Phil Read	Norton	95.10
	Lightweight 250cc	188¾	Mike Hailwood	Honda	98.38

Year	Race Class	Miles	Rider	Make	Mph
	Lightweight				
	125cc	113¼	Mike Hailwood	Honda	88.23
	Sidecar	113¼	Max Deubel	BMW	87.65
1962	Senior	226½	Gary Hocking	MV Agusta	103.51
	Junior	226½	Mike Hailwood	MV Agusta	99.59
	Lightweight 250cc	226½	Derek Minter	Honda	96.68
	Lightweight 125cc	113¼	Liugi Taveri	Honda	89.88
	50cc	72½	Ernst Degner	Suzuki	75.12
	Sidecar	113½	Chris Vincent	BSA	83.57
1963	Senior	226½	Mike Hailwood	MV	104.64
	Junior	226½	Jim Redman	Honda	94.91
	Lightweight 250cc	226½	Jim Redman	Honda	94.85
	Lightweight 125cc	113¼	Hugh R. Anderson	Suzuki	89.27
	50cc	113¼	Mitsuo Itoh	Suzuki	78.81
	Sidecar	113¼	Florian Camathias	FCS	88.38
1964	Senior	226½	Mike Hailwood	MV	100.95
	Junior	226½	Jim Redman	Honda	98.50
	Lightweight 250cc	226½	Jim Redman	Honda	97.45
	Lightweight 125cc	113¼	Luigi Taveri	Honda	92.14
	50cc	113¼	Hugh R. Anderson	Suzuki	80.64
	Sidecar	113¼	Max Duebel	BMW	89.12
1965	Senior	226½	Mike Hailwood	MV	91.69
	Junior	226½	Jim Redman	Honda	100.72
	Lightweight 250cc	226½	Jim Redman	Honda	97.19
	Lightweight 125cc	113¼	Phil Read	Yamaha	94.28
	50cc	113¼	Luigi Taveri	Honda	79.66
	Sidecar	113¼	Max Deubel	BMW	90.57
1966	Senior	226½	Mike Hailwood	Honda	103.11
	Junior	226½	Giacomo Agostini	MV	100.87
	Lightweight 250cc	226½	Mike Hailwood	Honda	101.79
	Lightweight 125cc	113¼	Bill Ivy	Yamaha	97.66
	50cc	113¼	Ralph Bryans	Honda	85.66
	Sidecar	113¼	Fritz Scheidegger	BMW	90.76

Year	Race Class	Miles	Rider	Make	Mph
1967	500cc	226½	Mike Hailwood	Honda	105.62
	350cc	226½	Mike Hailwood	Honda	104.68
	250cc	226½	Mike Hailwood	Honda	103.07
	125cc	113¼	Phil Read	Yamaha	97.48
	50cc	113¼	Stuart Graham	Suzuki	82.89
	Production 750cc	113¼	John Hartle	Triumph	97.10
	Production 500cc	113¼	Neil Kelly	Velocette	89.99
	Production 250cc	113¼	Bill Smith	Bultaco Metralla	88.63
	Sidecar	113¼	Siegfried Schauzu	BMW	90.96
1968	500cc	226½	Giacomo Agostini	MV	101.63
	350cc	226½	Giacomo Agostini	MV	104.78
	250cc	226½	Bill Ivy	Yamaha	99.58
	125cc	113¼	Phil Read	Yamaha	99.12
	50cc	113¼	Barry Smith	Derbi	72.90
	Production 750cc	113¼	Ray Pickrell	Dunstall	98.12
	Production 500cc	113¼	Ray Knight	Triumph	90.09
	Production 250cc	113¼	Trevor Burgess	Ossa	87.21
	Sidecar 750cc	113¼	Terry Vinicombe J. Flaxman	BSA	85.85
	Sidecar 500cc	113¼	Siegfried Schauzu H. Schneider	BMW	91.09
1969	500cc	226½	Giacomo Agostini	MV	104.75
	350cc	226½	Giacomo Agostini	MV	101.81
	250cc	226½	Kel Carruthers	Benelli	95.95
	125cc	113¼	Dave Simmonds	Kawasaki	91.08
	Production 750cc	113¼	Malcolm Uphill	Triumph	99.99
	Production 500cc	113¼	W. Graham Penny	Honda	88.18
	Production 250cc	113¼	Mike Rogers	Ducati	83.79
	Sidecar 750cc	113¼	Siegfried Schauzu H. Schneider	BMW	89.83
	Sidecar 500cc	113¼	Klaus Enders R. Engelhardt	BMW	92.48

Year	Race Class	Miles	Rider	Make	Mph
1970	500cc	226½	Giacomo Agostini	MV Agusta	101.52
	350cc	226½	Giacomo Agostini	MV Agusta	101.77
	250cc	226½	Kel Carruthers	Yamaha	96.13
	125cc	113¼	Dieter Braun	Suzuki	89.27
	Production 750cc	113¼	Malcolm Uphill	Trident	97.71
	Production 500cc	113¼	Frank Whiteway	Suzuki	89.94
	Production 250cc	113¼	Charles Mortimer	Ducati	84.87
	Sidecar 750cc	113¼	Siegfried Schauzu Horst Schneider	BMW	90.20
	Sidecar 500cc	113¼	Klaus Enders Wolfgang Kaluch	BMW	92.93
1971	750cc	113¼	Tony Jeffries	Triumph	102.85
	500cc	226½	Giacomo Agostini	MV Agusta	102.59
	350cc	188¾	Tony Jeffries	Yansel	89.98
	250cc	151	Phil Read	Yamaha	98.02
	125cc	113¼	Charles Mortimer	Yamaha	83.00
	Production 750cc	113¼	Ray Pickrell	BSA	100.07
	Production 500cc	113¼	John Williams	Honda	91.09
	Production 250cc	113¼	Bill Smith	Honda	84.20
	Sidecar 750cc	113¼	Georg Averbacher Herman Hahn	BMW	86.86
	Sidecar 500cc	113¼	Siegfried Schauzu Wolfgang Kaluch	BMW	86.21
1972	750cc	188¾	Ray Pickrell	Triumph	104.23
	500cc	188¾	Giacomo Agostini	MV	104.02
	350cc	188¾	Giacomo Agostini	MV	102.03
	250cc	151	Phil Read	Yamaha	99.68
	125cc	113¼	Charles Mortimer	Yamaha	87.49
	Production 750cc	151	Ray Pickrell	Triumph	100.00
	Production 500cc	151	Stan Woods	Suzuki	92.20
	Production 250cc	151	John Williams	Honda	85.32

Year	Race Class	Miles	Rider	Make	Mph
	Sidecar				
	750cc	113¼	Siegfried Schauzu Wolfgang Kaluch	BMW	90.97
	Sidecar				
	500cc	113¼	Siegfried Schauzu Wolfgang Kaluch	BMW	91.85
1973	750cc	188¾	Peter Williams	Norton	105.47
	500cc	188¾	Jack Findley	Suzuki	101.55
	350cc	188¾	Tony Rutter	Yamaha	101.99
	250cc	151	Charlie Williams	Yamaha	100.05
	125cc	113¼	Tommy Robb	Yamaha	89.90
	Production				
	750cc	151	Tony Jeffries	Triumph	95.62
	Production				
	500cc	151	Bill Smith	Honda	88.1
	Production				
	250cc	151	Charlie Williams	Yamaha	81.67
	Sidecar				
	750cc	113¼	Klaus Enders Rolf Englehardt	BMW	
	Sidecar				
	500cc	113¼	Klaus Enders Rolf Englehardt	BMW	94.93

International Six-Day Trials champions

1913	Great Britain	1937	Great Britain
1920	Switzerland	1938	Great Britain
1921	Switzerland	1939	Results not approved by
1922	Switzerland		the FIM
1923	Sweden	1947	Czechoslovakia
1924	Great Britain	1948	Great Britain
1925	Great Britain	1949	Great Britain
1926	Great Britain	1950	Great Britain
1927	Great Britain	1951	Great Britain
1928	Great Britain	1952	Czechoslovakia
1929	Great Britain	1953	Czechoslovakia
1930	Italy	1954	Czechoslovakia
1931	Italy	1955	West Germany
1932	Great Britain	1956	Czechoslovakia
1933	Germany	1957	West Germany
1934	Germany	1958	Czechoslovakia
1935	Germany	1959	Czechoslovakia
1936	Great Britain	1960	Austria

1961	West Germany	1968	West Germany
1962	Czechoslovakia	1969	East Germany
1963	East Germany	1970	Czechoslovakia
1964	East Germany	1971	Czechoslovakia
1965	East Germany	1972	Czechoslovakia
1966	East Germany	1973	Czechoslovakia
1967	East Germany		

SUMMARY:

Victories—Great Britain, 15; Czechoslovakia, 12; East Germany, 6; West Germany, 4; Germany, 3; Switzerland, 3; Italy, 2; Sweden, 1; Austria, 1.

World Speedway champions

1936	Lionel Van Praag (Australia)	1960	Ove Fundin (Sweden)
1937	Jack Milne (USA)	1961	Ove Fundin (Sweden)
1938	"Bluey" Wilkinson	1962	Peter Craven (England)
	(Australia)	1963	Ove Fundin (Sweden)
1949	Tommy Price (England)	1964	Barry Briggs (New Zealand)
1950	Fred Williams (Wales)	1965	Bjorn Knutsson (Sweden)
1951	Jack Young (Australia)	1966	Barry Briggs (New Zealand)
1952	Jack Young (Australia)	1967	Ove Fundin (Sweden)
1953	Fred Williams (Wales)	1968	Ivan Mauger (New Zealand)
1954	Ronnie Moore (New Zealand)	1969	Ivan Mauger (New Zealand)
1955	Peter Craven (England)	1970	Ivan Mauger (New Zealand)
1956	Ove Fundin (Sweden)	1971	Ole Olsen (Denmark)
1957	Barry Briggs (New Zealand)	1972	Ivan Mauger (New Zealand)
1958	Barry Briggs (New Zealand)	1973	Jerzy Szczakiel (Poland)
1959	Ronnie Moore (New Zealand)		

SUMMARY:

Tally of victories—New Zealand, 10; Sweden, 6; Australia, 4; England, 3; Wales, 2; USA, 1; Denmark, 1; Poland, 1.
Most wins by rider—Ove Fundin, 5.

AMA Grand National champions

Date	Rider	Location	Cycle
1946	Chet Dygraaf	Grand Rapids, Mich.	Norton
1947	Jimmy Chann	Bridgeton, N.J.	Harley-Davidson
1948	Jimmy Chann	Bridgeton, N.J.	Harley-Davidson
1949	Jimmy Chann	Bridgeton, N.J.	Harley-Davidson
1950	Larry Headrick	San Jose, Cal.	Harley-Davidson
1951	Bobby Hill	Columbus, O.	Indian

Date	Rider	Country	Cycle
1952	Bobby Hill	Columbus, O.	Indian
1953	Bill Tuman	Rock Island, Ill.	Indian
1954	Joe Leonard	San Jose, Cal.	Harley-Davidson
1955	Brad Andres	San Diego, Cal.	Harley-Davidson
1956	Joe Leonard	San Jose, Cal.	Harley-Davidson
1957	Joe Leonard	San Jose, Cal.	Harley-Davidson
1958	Carroll Resweber	Cedarburg, Wis.	Harley-Davidson
1959	Carroll Resweber	Cedarburg, Wis.	Harley-Davidson
1960	Carroll Resweber	Cedarburg, Wis.	Harley-Davidson
1961	Carroll Resweber	Cedarburg, Wis.	Harley-Davidson
1962	Bart Markel	Flint, Mich.	Harley-Davidson
1963	Dick Mann	Richmond, Cal.	BSA Matchless
1964	Roger Reiman	Kewanee, Ill.	Harley-Davidson
1965	Bart Markel	Flint, Mich.	Harley-Davidson
1966	Bart Markel	Flint, Mich.	Harley-Davidson
1967	Gary Nixon	Phoenix, Md.	Triumph
1968	Gary Nixon	Phoenix, Md.	Triumph
1969	Mert Lawwill	San Francisco, Cal.	Harley-Davidson
1970	Gene Romero	San Louis Obispo, Cal.	Triumph
1971	Dick Mann	Richmond, Cal.	BSA
1972	Mark Brelsford	Woodside, Cal.	Harley-Davidson
1973	Kenny Roberts	Woodside, Cal.	Yamaha

SUMMARY:
Most championships—Carroll Resweber, 4.
Best manufacturer record—Harley-Davidson, 18.

World Moto-Cross champions

Date	Rider	Country	Cycle
250cc			
1957	Fritz Betzebacher	West Germany	Maico
1958	Jaromir Cizek	Czechoslovakia	Jawa (CZ)
1959	Rolf Tibblin	Sweden	Husqvarna
1960	Dave Bickers	England	Greeves
1961	Dave Bickers	England	Greeves
1962	Torsten Hallman	Sweden	Husqvarna
1963	Torsten Hallman	Sweden	Husqvarna
1964	Joel Robert	Belgium	CZ
1965	Viktor Arbekov	USSR	CZ
1966	Torsten Hallman	Sweden	Husqvarna
1967	Torsten Hallman	Sweden	Husqvarna
1968	Joel Robert	Belgium	CZ
1969	Joel Robert	Belgium	CZ

Date	Rider	Country	Cycle
1970	Joel Robert	Belgium	Suzuki
1971	Joel Robert	Belgium	Suzuki
1972	Joel Robert	Belgium	Suzuki
1973	Hakan Andersson	Sweden	Yamaha

500cc

Date	Rider	Country	Cycle
1952	Victor Leloup	Belgium	FN
1953	Auguste Mingels	Belgium	FN
1954	Auguste Mingels	Belgium	FN
1955	John Draper	England	BSA
1956	Les Archer	England	Norton
1957	Bill Nilsson	Sweden	AJS
1958	Rene Baeten	Belgium	FN
1959	Sten Lundin	Sweden	Monark
1960	Bill Nilsson	Sweden	Husqvarna
1961	Sten Lundin	Sweden	Monark
1962	Rolf Tibblin	Sweden	Husqvarna
1963	Rolf Tibblin	Sweden	Husqvarna
1964	Jeff Smith	England	BSA
1965	Jeff Smith	England	BSA
1966	Paul Friedrichs	East Germany	CZ
1967	Paul Friedrichs	East Germany	CZ
1968	Paul Friedrich	East Germany	CZ
1969	Bengt Aberg	Sweden	Husqvarna
1970	Bengt Aberg	Sweden	Husqvarna
1971	Roger DeCoster	Belgium	Suzuki
1972	Roger DeCoster	Belgium	Suzuki
1973	Roger DeCoster	Belgium	Suzuki

SUMMARY:

Most victories by manufacturer—Husqvarna, 10; CZ, 8; Suzuki, 5.
Most victories by rider—Joel Robert, 6; Torsten Hallman, 4.
Most victories by country—Sweden, 14; Belgium, 13; England, 6.

World Motorcycle Road Racing champions

Date	Rider	Country	Cycle

50cc

Date	Rider	Country	Cycle
1962	Ernst Degner	West Germany	Suzuki
1963	Hugh R. Anderson	New Zealand	Suzuki
1964	Hugh R. Anderson	New Zealand	Suzuki
1965	Ralph Bryans	Ireland	Honda
1966	Hans Anscheidt	West Germany	Suzuki

Date	Rider	Country	Cycle
1967	Hans Anscheidt	West Germany	Suzuki
1968	Hans Anscheidt	West Germany	Suzuki
1969	Angelo Nieto	Spain	Derbi
1970	Angelo Nieto	Spain	Derbi
1971	Jan De Vries	Netherlands	Kriedler
1972	Jan De Vries	Netherlands	Kreidler
1973	Jan De Vries	Netherlands	Kreidler

125cc

Date	Rider	Country	Cycle
1949	Nello Pagani	Italy	MV Agusta
1950	B. Ruffo	Italy	MV Agusta
1951	Carlo Ubbiali	Italy	MV Agusta
1952	Cecil Sandford	England	MV Agusta
1953	Werner Haas	West Germany	NSU
1954	Rupert Hollaus	Austria	NSU
1955	Carlo Ubbiali	Italy	MV Agusta
1956	Carlo Ubbiali	Italy	MV Agusta
1957	Tarquinio Provini	Italy	Mondial
1958	Carlo Ubbiali	Italy	MV Agusta
1959	Carlo Ubbiali	Italy	MV Agusta
1960	Carlo Ubbiali	Italy	MV Agusta
1961	Tom Phillis	Australia	Honda
1962	Luigi Taveri	Switzerland	Honda
1963	Hugh R. Anderson	New Zealand	Suzuki
1964	Luigi Taveri	Switzerland	Honda
1965	Hugh R. Anderson	New Zealand	Suzuki
1966	Luigi Taveri	Switzerland	Honda
1967	Bill Ivy	England	Yamaha
1968	Phil Read	England	Yamaha
1969	Dave Simmonds	England	Kawasaki
1970	Dieter Braun	West Germany	Suzuki
1971	Angelo Nieto	Spain	Derbi
1972	Angelo Nieto	Spain	Derbi
1973	Kent Andersson	Sweden	Yamaha

250cc

Date	Rider	Country	Cycle
1949	B. Ruffo	Italy	Moto-Guzzi
1950	Dario Ambrosini	Italy	Benelli
1951	B. Ruffo	Italy	Moto-Guzzi
1952	E. Lorenzetti	Italy	Moto-Guzzi
1953	Werner Haas	West Germany	NSU
1954	Werner Haas	West Germany	NSU
1955	H. P. Muller	West Germany	NSU

Date	Rider	Country	Cycle
1956	Carlo Ubbiali	Italy	MV Agusta
1957	Cecil Sandford	England	Mondial
1958	Tarquinio Provini	Italy	MV Agusta
1959	Carlo Ubbiali	Italy	MV Agusta
1960	Carlo Ubbiali	Italy	MV Agusta
1961	Mike Hailwood	England	Honda
1962	Jim Redman	Southern Rhodesia	Honda
1963	Jim Redman	Southern Rhodesia	Honda
1964	Phil Read	England	Yamaha
1965	Phil Read	England	Yamaha
1966	Mike Hailwood	England	Honda
1967	Mike Hailwood	England	Honda
1968	Phil Read	England	Yamaha
1969	Kel Carruthers	Australia	Benelli
1970	Rod Gould	England	Yamaha
1971	Phil Read	England	Yamaha
1972	Jarno Saarinen	Finland	Yamaha
1973	Dieter Braun	West Germany	Yamaha

350cc

Date	Rider	Country	Cycle
1949	Freddie Frith	England	Velocette
1950	J. R. Foster	England	Velocette
1951	Geoff Duke	England	Norton
1952	Geoff Duke	England	Norton
1953	Fergus Anderson	England	Moto-Guzzi
1954	Fergus Anderson	England	Moto-Guzzi
1955	Bill Lomas	England	Moto-Guzzi
1956	Bill Lomas	England	Moto-Guzzi
1957	Keith Campbell	Australia	Moto-Guzzi
1958	John Surtees	England	MV Agusta
1959	John Surtees	England	MV Agusta
1960	John Surtees	England	MV Agusta
1961	Gary Hocking	Southern Rhodesia	MV Agusta
1962	Jim Redman	Southern Rhodesia	Honda
1963	Jim Redman	Southern Rhodesia	Honda
1964	Jim Redman	Southern Rhodesia	Honda
1965	Jim Redman	Southern Rhodesia	Honda
1966	Mike Hailwood	England	MV Agusta
1967	Mike Hailwood	England	Honda
1968	Giacomo Agostini	Italy	MV Agusta
1969	Giacomo Agostini	Italy	MV Agusta
1970	Giacomo Agostini	Italy	MV Agusta
1971	Giacomo Agostini	Italy	MV Agusta
1972	Giacomo Agostini	Italy	MV Agusta
1973	Giacomo Agostini	Italy	MV Agusta

Date	Rider	Location	Cycle
500cc			
1949	Les Graham	England	AJS
1950	Umberto Masetti	Italy	Gilera
1951	Geoff Duke	England	Norton
1952	Umberto Masetti	Italy	Gilera
1953	Geoff Duke	England	Gilera
1954	Geoff Duke	England	Gilera
1955	Geoff Duke	England	Gilera
1956	John Surtees	England	MV Agusta
1957	Libero Liberati	Italy	Gilera
1958	John Surtees	England	MV Agusta
1959	John Surtees	England	MV Agusta
1960	John Surtees	England	MV Agusta
1961	Gary Hocking	Southern Rhodesia	MV Agusta
1962	Mike Hailwood	England	MV Agusta
1963	Mike Hailwood	England	MV Agusta
1964	Mike Hailwood	England	MV Agusta
1965	Mike Hailwood	England	MV Agusta
1966	Giacomo Agostini	Italy	MV Agusta
1967	Giacomo Agostini	Italy	MV Agusta
1968	Giacomo Agostini	Italy	MV Agusta
1969	Giacomo Agostini	Italy	MV Agusta
1970	Giacomo Agostini	Italy	MV Agusta
1971	Giacomo Agostini	Italy	MV Agusta
1972	Giacomo Agostini	Italy	MV Agusta
1973	Phil Read	England	MV Agusta

500cc Sidecars

Date	Rider	Location	Cycle
1949	Eric Oliver	England	Norton
1950	Eric Oliver	England	Norton
1951	Eric Oliver	England	Norton
1952	Cyril Smith	England	Norton
1953	Eric Oliver	England	Norton
1954	Willi Noll	West Germany	BMW
1955	Werner Faust	West Germany	BMW
1956	Willi Noll	West Germany	BMW
1957	Fritz Hillebrand	West Germany	BMW
1958	Willy Schneider	West Germany	BMW
1959	Willy Schneider	West Germany	BMW
1960	Helmut Fath	West Germany	BMW
1961	Max Deubel	West Germany	BMW
1962	Max Deubel	West Germany	BMW
1963	No champion		
1964	Max Deubel	West Germany	BMW
1965	Fritz Scheidegger	Switzerland	BMW

Date	Rider	Location	Cycle
1966	Fritz Scheidegger	Switzerland	BMW
1967	Klaus Enders	West Germany	BMW
1968	Helmut Fath	West Germany	URS
1969	Klaus Enders	West Germany	BMW
1970	Klaus Enders	West Germany	BMW
1971	Horst Owesle	West Germany	Munch
1972	Klaus Enders	West Germany	BMW
1973	Klaus Enders	West Germany	BMW

SUMMARY:

Tally of victories—MV Agusta, 41; BMW, 17; Honda, 15; Yamaha, 10; Suzuki, 9; Moto-Guzzi, 8; Norton, 8.

Most championships by rider—Giacomo Agostini, 13; Mike Hailwood, 9; Carlo Ubbiali, 9; John Surtees, 7.

Most wins by country—England, 45; Italy, 33; West Germany, 27.

World Ice Racing champions

1966	Gadbrhman (Beatle) Kadyrov, USSR
1967	Boris Samorodov, USSR
1968	Gadbrhman (Beatle) Kadyrov, USSR
1969	Gadbrhman (Beatle) Kadyrov, USSR
1970	Antonin Svab, USSR
1971	Gadbrhman (Beatle) Kadyrov, USSR
1972	Gadbrhman (Beatle) Kadyrov, USSR
1973	Gadbrhman (Beatle) Kadyrov, USSR
1974	Milan Spinka, Czechoslovakia

Daytona Motorcycle Classic champions

Year	Rider	Make	Mph

200-Mile Expert Championship

Year	Rider	Make	Mph
1937	Ed Kretz, Monterey Park, Cal.	Indian	73.34
1938	Ben Campanale, Pomona, Cal.	Harley-Davidson	73.99
1939	Ben Campanale, Pomona, Cal.	Harley-Davidson	76.68
1940	Babe Tancrede, Woonsocket, R.I.	Harley-Davidson	75.11
1941	Billy Mathews, Hamilton, Ont., Canada	Norton	78.08
1947	Johnny Spiegelhoff, Milwaukee, Wis.	Indian	77.14
1948	Floyd Emde, San Diego, Cal.	Indian	74.01
1949	Dick Klamfoth, Groveport, O.	Norton	86.42
1950	Billy Mathews, Hamilton, Ont., Canada	Norton	88.55
1951	Dick Klamfoth, Groveport, O.	Norton	92.81

Year	Rider	Make	Mph
1952	Dick Klamfoth, Groveport, O.	Norton	87.71
1953	Paul Goldsmith, St. Clair Shores, Mich.	Harley-Davidson	94.25
1954	Bobby Hill, Columbus, O.	BSA	94.24
1955	Brad Andres, San Diego, Cal.	Harley-Davidson	94.57
1956	John Gibson, Duarte, Cal.	Harley-Davidson	94.21
1957	Joe Leonard, San Jose, Cal.	Harley-Davidson	98.52
1958	Joe Leonard, San Jose, Cal.	Harley-Davidson	99.86
1959	Brad Andres, San Diego, Cal.	Harley-Davidson	98.70
1960	Brad Andres, San Diego, Cal.	Harley-Davidson	98.06
1961	Roger Reiman, Kewanee, Ill.	Harley-Davidson	69.25
1962	Don Burnett, Danvers, Mass.	Triumph	71.981
1963	Ralph White, San Diego, Cal.	Harley-Davidson	77.678
1964	Roger Reiman, Kewanee, Ill.	Harley-Davidson	94.833
1965	Roger Reiman, Kewanee, Ill.	Harley-Davidson	90.041
1966	Buddy Elmore, El Paso, Tex.	Triumph	96.582
1967	Gary Nixon, Baltimore, Md.	Triumph	98.227
1968	Calvin Rayborn, San Diego, Cal.	Harley-Davidson	101.290
1969	Calvin Rayborn, San Diego, Cal.	Harley-Davidson	100.882
1970	Dick Mann, Richmond, Cal.	Honda	102.69
1971	Dick Mann, Richmond, Cal.	BSA	104.71
1972	Don Emde, San Diego, Cal.	Yamaha	103.358
1973	Jarno Saarinan, Finland	Yamaha	98.178
1974	Giacomo Agostini, Italy	Yamaha	105.005

100-Mile Junior Winners

Year	Rider	Make	Mph
1947	Jack Horn, Rosamond, Cal.	Indian	73.35
1948	Don Evans, San Bernardino, Cal.	Norton	75.50
1949	Don Evans, San Bernardino, Cal.	Norton	79.73
1950	Rod Coates, Plainfield, N.J.	Triumph	81.24
1951	Bob Michael, Pomona, Cal.	Norton	82.54
1952	Cancelled, rain. (Note: A 50-miler was held in 1953 to make up for this race. Winner was Nick Nicholson, Long Beach, Cal., riding a BSA; average speed, 93.99).		
1953	John Miller, Ft. Thomas, Ky.	Norton	90.74
1954	Bobby Stilwell, Houston, Tex.	Triumph	93.26
1955	Dan Richards, Little Rock, Ark.	Harley-Davidson	92.43
1956	Bates Molyneaux, Corpus Christi, Tex.	Harley-Davidson	93.58
1957	Kenny Brown, Covina, Cal.	BSA	93.87
1958	Larry Schafer, Sarasota, Fla.	Harley-Davidson	95.21
1959	Bill Scott, Kewanee, Ill.	Harley-Davidson	no speed
1960	Tom Segraves, Orlando, Fla.	Harley-Davidson	97.05
1961	Jody Nicholas, Nashville, Tenn.	BSA	69.76
1962	George Montgomery, Mt. Vernon, N.Y.	BSA	68.601
1963	Buddy Stubbs, Bellflower, Cal.	Harley-Davidson	73.224
1964	Kenneth Hayes, Johnson City, Tenn.	Norton	90.908

Year	Rider	Make	Mph
1965	Wayne Cook, Richmond, Va.	Harley-Davidson	92.430
1966	Kenneth Ridder, San Francisco, Cal.	Harley-Davidson	91.350
1967	Walter Fulton, Orange, Cal.	Harley-Davidson	94.000
1968	Bill Lyons, San Francisco, Cal.	Honda	94.140
1969	Ronald Muir, Dowell, Ill.	Yamaha	96.10
1970	Rusty Bradley, Austin, Tex.	Kawasaki	100.723
1971	Dennis Poneleit, Sarasota, Fla.	Honda	99.925
1972	Ronnie Dottley, Birmingham, Ala.	Yamaha	103.316
1973	Phil McDonald, Sapulpa, Okla.	Yamaha	96.665
1974	Pat Hennen, San Mateo, Cal.	Yamaha	102.193

76-Mile Novice Race

Year	Rider	Make	Mph
1962	Howard Utsley, Washington, D.C.	BSA	67.869
1963	Edward Moran, Farmingdale, N.J.	BSA	72.927
1964	James Faulkerson, Menlo Park, Cal.	Yamaha	87.355
1965	Sonny Gager, Jacksonville, Fla.	Honda	85.008
1966	Walter Fulton, Orange, Cal.	Suzuki	89.122
1967	Kenneth Stephens, Sarasota, Fla.	Yamaha	88.868
1968	Don Hollingsworth, St. Augustine, Fla.	Harley-Davidson	92.982
1969	Harry Cone, Sherman, Tex.	Yamaha	93.530
1970	Jerry Christopher, West Covina, Cal.	Yamaha	94.395
1971	Howard Lynggard, Buena Park, Cal.	Yamaha	96.40
1972	Johnny Long, Miami, Fla.	Yamaha	99.718
1973	Gary Blackman, Emmaus, Pa.	Yamaha	92.804
1974	John Volkman, Seal Beach, Cal.	Yamaha	94.978

100-Mile Combined Junior and Expert Race

Year	Rider	Make	Mph
1963	Dick Hammer, Lakewood, Cal.	Harley-Davidson	71.490
1964	Dick Hammer, Lakewood, Cal.	Harley-Davidson	88.455
1965	Dick Mann, Crockett, Cal.	Yamaha	91.606
1966	Bob Winters, Ft. Smith, Ark.	Yamaha	91.876
1967	Gary Nixon, Baltimore, Md.	Yamaha	94.094
1968	Yvon du Hamel, Montreal, Que., Canada	Yamaha	96.253
1969	Yvon du Hamel, Montreal, Que., Canada	Yamaha	98.384
1970	Kel Carruthers, Australia	Yamaha	101.721
1971	Kel Carruthers, Australia	Yamaha	102.14
1972	Dave Smith, Lakewood, Cal.	Yamaha	101.497
1973	Gary Fisher, Parkesburg, Pa.	Yamaha	95.787
1974	Don Castro, Hollister, Cal.	Yamaha	99.018

motorcycles available in the United States

AJS
Triumph Norton, Inc.
2745 E. Huntington Dr.
Duarte, Cal. 91010
Area 213 531-7138

Berliner Motor Corp.
Railroad St. and Plant Rd.
Hasbrouck Heights, N.J. 07604
Area 201 288-9696

APACHE
Apache, Ltd.
110 E. Santa Anita Ave.
Burbank, Cal. 91502
Area 213 843-4633

ATTEX
ATV Manufacturing Co.
1215 William Flynn Hwy.
Route 8
Glenshaw, Pa. 15116
Area 412 782-5523

BENELLI
Cosmopolitan Motors, Inc.
Jacksonville and Meadowbrook Rds.
Hatboro, Pa. 19040
Area 215 672-9100

BIRD
Bird Engineering
P.O. Box J
Freemont, Neb. 68025
Area 402 721-8250

BMW
Butler & Smith, Inc.
Walnut St. and Hudson Ave.
Norwood, N.J. 07648
Area 201 767-1223

Butler & Smith, Inc.
135 E. Stanley St.
Compton, Cal. 90220
Area 213 638-8508

BRIDGESTONE
Rockford Motors, Inc.
1911 Harrison Ave.
Rockford, Ill. 61108
Area 815 398-1220

BRONCO
Engine Specialties, Inc.
P.O. Box 260
Cornwell Heights, Pa. 19020
Area 215 785-3232 or 639-6500

BULTACO
Bultaco International
5447 Greenwich Rd.
Virginia Beach, Va. 23462
Area 801 499-8501

Bultaco American West
2765 Scott Blvd.
Santa Clara, Cal. 95052
Area 408 241-4672

CAN-AM
Bombardier, Ltd.
Valcourt, P.Q.
CANADA
Area 514 232-2211

CAPRIOLA
Cosmopolitan Motors, Inc.
Jacksonville and Meadowbrook Rds.
Hatboro, Pa. 19040
Area 215 672-9100

CARABELA
Carabela West
16756 Foothill Blvd.
Fontana, Cal. 92335
Area 714 822-1056

Carabela East
131 S. Detroit
Bellefontaine, O. 43311
Area 513 593-8226

CAT

HPE Muskin Corp.
225 Acacia St.
Colton, Cal. 92324
Area 714 825-8200

CHAPARRAL

Chaparral Motorcycle Corp.
5995 N. Washington St.
Denver, Colo. 80216
Area 303 292-1240

COOPER

Cooper Motors
110 E. Santa Anita Ave.
Burbank, Cal. 91502
Area 213 843-4633

CZ

American Jawa, Ltd.
185 Express St.
Plainview, N.Y. 11803
Area 516 938-3210

American Jawa, Ltd.
18408 Laurel Park Rd.
Compton, Cal. 90224
Area 213 537-8400

Union Sales Distributing Co.
630 N. Witchduck Rd.
Virginia Beach, Va. 23462
Area 804 499-8961

DALESMAN

Jeckel Industries, Inc.
38 Everts Ave.
Glen Falls, N.Y. 12801
Area 518 793-5181

DKW

Hercules Distributing Co.
9827 Mason Ave.
Chatsworth, Cal. 91311
Area 213 882-8272

DUCATI

Berliner Motor Corp.
Railroad St. and Plant Rd.
Hasbrouck Heights, N.Y. 07604
Area 201 288-9696

DUNE CYCLE

Allied Mechanical Products
Division of Tower Industries
13623 Pumice St.
Santa Fe Springs, Cal. 90670
Area 213 921-6675

ESO

American Jawa, Ltd.
185 Express St.
Plainview, N.Y. 11803
Area 516 938-3210

American Jawa, Ltd.
18408 Laurel Park Rd.
Compton, Cal. 90224
Area 213 537-8400

Union Sales Distributing Co.
630 N. Witchduck Rd.
Virginia Beach, Va. 23462
Area 804 499-8961

GEMINI

San Tong Co.
15514 S. Figueroa St.
Gardena, Cal. 90247
Area 213 532-1780

GREEVES

R. G. Wilson
P.O. Box 54 Greendale Station
Worcester, Mass. 01606
Area 617 869-2016

Nick Nicholson Motors
11629 Van Owen St.
North Hollywood, Cal. 91605
Area 213 764-8674

GRINGO

Power-Dyne Vehicles, Inc.
Jenks Hill Rd.
Lincoln, R.I. 02865
Area 401 728-2900

185   Motorcycles Available in the United States

HARLEY-DAVIDSON
AMF/Harley-Davidson Motor Co.
3700 W. Juneau Ave.
Milwaukee, Wis. 53201
Area 414 342-4680

HODAKA
Pabatco
327 Sherman Rd.
Athena, Ore. 97813
Area 503 566-3526

Penartic Distributing Co.
Star Route Box 59
Lock Haven, Pa. 17745
Area 717 769-6482

Northeast Hodaka
17 Main St.
Holden, Mass. 01520
Area 617 829-3987

Tiger Distributing Co.
653 W. Broadway
Glendale, Cal. 91204
Area 213 246-7132

HOLDER
Die Cast Finishing Co.
2020 Lakeside Ave.
Cleveland, O. 44114
Area 216 696-6070

HONDA
American Honda Motor Co.
100 W. Alondra Blvd.
Gardena, Cal. 90247
Area 213 321-8680

HUSQVARNA
Husqvarna West
4935 Mercury St.
San Diego, Cal. 92111
Area 714 565-1414

Husqvarna East
1906 Broadway Ave.
Lorain, O. 74051
Area 216 244-1515

INDIAN
Indian Motorcycles, Inc.
110 N. Doheny Dr.
Beverly Hills, Cal. 90211
Area 213 278-9470

ISLO
Grapevine Racing Motors
750 E. Pawnee
Wichita, Kan. 67211
Area 316 733-1901

JAWA
American Jawa, Ltd.
185 Express St.
Plainview, N.Y. 11803
Area 516 938-3210

American Jawa, Ltd.
18408 Laurel Park Rd.
Compton, Cal. 90224
Area 213 537-8400

Union Sales Distributing Co.
630 N. Witchduck Rd.
Virginia Beach, Va. 23462
Area 804 499-8961

KAMI
Kami Sales Corp.
2750-M Oregon Ct.
Torrance, Cal. 90503
Area 213 320-3700

KAWASAKI
Kawasaki Motors Corp. U.S.A.
1062 McGaw Ave.
Santa Ana, Cal. 92705
Area 714 540-9980

Kawasaki Motors Corp. U.S.A.
13 Production Way
Avenal, N.J. 07001
Area 201 381-0800

Kawasaki Motors Corp. U.S.A.
6104 Boat Rock Blvd. S.W.
Atlanta, Ga. 30336
Area 404 349-2000

Kawasaki Motors Corp. U.S.A.
1710 111th St.
Grand Prairie, Tex. 75050
Area 214 263-5761

Kawasaki Motors Corp. U.S.A.
14225 25th Ave. North
Minneapolis, Minn. 55441
Area 612 546-5341

LAVERDA
Continental Motorcycles
150 Ludlow Ave.
Northvale, N.J. 07647
Area 201 767-3673

MAICO
Eastern Maico
Royal and Duke Sts.
Reedsville, Pa. 17084
Area 717 667-3987

Debenhan Imports
887 Main St.
Antioch, Ill. 60002
Area 312 395-2100

Cooper Motors
110 E. Santa Anita Ave.
Burbank, Cal. 91502
Area 213 843-4633

MONARK
Inter-Trends
3001 Red Hills Ave.
Costa Mesa, Cal. 92626
Area 714 979-1550

MONTESA
Montesa Motors, Inc.
3657 W. Beverly Blvd.
Los Angeles, Cal. 90004
Area 213 663-8258

MOTO-GUZZI
Premiere Motor Corp.
Railroad St. and Plant Rd.
Hasbrouck Heights, N.J. 07604
Area 201 288-9694

ZDS Motor Corp.
4655 San Fernando Rd.
Glendale, Cal. 91204
Area 213 245-8695

MV AGUSTA
Ed LaBelle Cycle Engineering
15 Calconhook Rd.
Sharon Hill, Pa. 19079
Area 215 586-2060

MZ
International Accessories East
102 Park St.
Hampshire, Ill. 60140
Area 312 683-3865

International Accessories West
4225 30th St.
San Diego, Cal. 92104
Area 714 280-3344

NORTON
Triumph Norton, Inc.
2745 E. Huntington Dr.
Duarte, Cal. 91010
Area 213 531-7138

Berliner Motor Corp.
Railroad St. and Plant Rd.
Hasbrouck Heights, N.J. 07604
Area 201 288-9696

OSSA
Yankee Motor Corp.
P.O. Box 36
Schnectady, N.Y. 12306
Area 518 372-4726

PENTON
Penton Imports
3709 W. Erie Ave.
Lorain, O. 44053
Area 216 244-4101

Penton West
9604 Oates Dr.
Sacramento, Cal. 95827
Area 916 362-4124

187 Motorcycles Available in the United States

PUCH

American Puch Distributing Co. East
148 W. Lancaster Ave.
Dowington, Pa. 19335
Area 215 269-3923

Puch Distributing Corp.
9825 Mason Ave.
Chatsworth, Cal. 91311
Area 213 882-8860

RICKMAN

Triumph Norton, Inc.
2745 E. Huntington Dr.
Duarte, Cal. 91010
Area 213 531-7138

Rickman, Inc.
2640 Merchant Dr.
Baltimore, Md. 21204
Area 301 525-3666

ROKON

Rokon, Inc.
160 Emerald St.
Keene, N.H. 03431
Area 603 352-7341

RUPP

Rupp Manufacturing Co.
1776 Airport Rd.
Mansfield, O. 44903
Area 419 522-5732

SPEEDWAY SPORTCYCLES

Speedway Products, Inc.
160 E. Longview Ave.
Mansfield, O. 44905
Area 419 522-5078

SUZUKI

U.S. Suzuki Motor Corp.
13767 Freeway Dr.
Santa Fe Springs, Cal. 90670
Area 213 921-4461

TAKA

Rockford Motors, Inc.
1911 Harrison Ave.
Rockford, Ill. 61108
Area 815 398-1220

TRIUMPH

Triumph Norton, Inc.
2745 E. Huntington Dr.
Duarte, Cal. 91010
Area 213 531-7138

TYRAN

Mitsubishi Corp.
124 Leuning St.
South Hackensack, N.J. 07606
Area 201 342-3600

VESPA

Western Scooter Distributors Corp.
1599 Custer Ave.
San Francisco, Cal. 94124
Area 415 647-5520

YAMAHA

Yamaha International Corp.
6600 Orangethorpe Ave.
Buena Park, Cal. 90620
Area 714 522-9011

YANKEE

Yankee Motor Corp.
P.O. Box 36
Schnectady, N.Y. 12306
Area 518 372-4726

Index

obstacle course, 31, 49–50
off-road riding, 29, 45, 145, 155, 163–64
    hazards, 57–61, 83, 89, 96–104
Off-Road Vehicle Advisory Committee.
    See public land
oil, 39–40, 80–82, 89
"On Any Sunday," 125
open land, closing of, to motor-cyclists,
    59, 98–101. *See also* public land
Otto, N. A., 5
overtaking vehicles, 57, 68
owner's manual, 24, 47, 86, 89

pacer motorcycles, 14, 113–14
Parkhurst, Red, 119, 121
parking, 161
parks, 103–106
Parkyns, Thomas, 6
passengers, 76–78, 91–92, 94, 163
    effect on steering, 76–77
Pennington, E. J., 9–12
Penton, John, 142
Petrali, Joe, 113, 122
physical fitness, 73
piston displacement, 16, 33
piston rings, 89
police use of motorcycles, 53–54, 65,
    148–49, 161–62
Potter, E. J., 152
power-to-weight ratio, 33, 84
protective clothing, 34–37, 69–70, 74–
    76, 91–93
public land, uses of, 100–104
    checkerboarding, 101–102
    restricted areas, 101
purchasing a motorcycle, 21–41
    long-range usability, 22, 24
    price-shopping, 24–25, 34, 163

racing, 112–139
    amateur competition, 136–37
    bike specifications, 31–33
    how to get into, 138–39
    professional competition, 137–38
Rayborn, Cal, 125, 135–39
rear shocks, 29–30
rearview mirror, 37, 94
registration, 45, 64, 93
repairs. *See* maintenance
Resweber, Carroll, 112–13
rider training school, 42–45, 48–51. *See*
    also educational programs; instruc-
    tion in riding
riding techniques, 49, 59, 137
road racing, 31, 138–39
Road Research Laboratory of Great
    Britain, 78
road surface, hazards of, 53, 55, 65–67
Roberts, J. N., 73
Robertson, Bill, Jr., 145
Rockwood, Roxy, 144
Rolfe, Walter, 147
Roots, J. D., 9
Roper, Sylvester H., 5–6

safety, 34, 42, 44, 51–52, 63–65, **78,**
    90–94, 155
    tips, 53–62, 65–72
Sanford, Russ, 94
Sarossy, Tibor, 143–44
seat, 28, 33, 39, 160–62
secondhand motorcycles, 39–41
selection of motorcycle. *See* purchasing
Serpollet, Leon, 7
service, 25–27, 79
Shimazu, Narazo, 19
short track racing, 132, 137
size. *See* engines, sizes of; weight;
    wheelbase
Smithsonian Institution, 5, 7

SNELL 1970 standard, 34
spark plugs, 82, 89, 98
speed
    of early motorcycles, 5–6, 12, 15
    high, 32–33, 69. *See also* racing
    low, 29–31
speedway racing, 127, 131–33, 137
stability, 33, 38, 161
"State of the Art of Traffic Safety, The," 64
steamcycle, 2–7
Stoddard Valley, 102
street bikes, 27–29, 83
street scrambler, 30
Streiff, William P., 147
stunt riding, 149–54
Sullivan, Ralph, 119
suspension systems, 29, 31, 62

T

Tanner, Sammy, 22–23, 68
Taylor, Ike, 147–48
Temple, Claude, 124, 135
theft, 106–108
Thomas, Jess, 135
Thomas, Parry, 124
Three Flags Run, 144
three-wheelers, 1–9, 160–63. *See also*
    Cynophere; Trigano
throttle, 9, 47–48, 68–69
Tice, M., 119
tires, 12
    maintenance, 65, 88
    for specialized bikes, 28–29, 32,
    39, 121, 137
Toms, Douglas, 91
torque, 24, 29, 31–32
Tourist Trophy bike, 32
traction, loss of, 69
traffic citations, 108–11
    handling the defense, 109–11
trail bikes, 30, 81
Trans-AMA series, 131
transmission, 14, 17, 39, 49–51, 163.
    See also gearshift

Tremulis, Alex, 135, 158–62
Trevithick, Richard, 3
trials, 31, 136
Triber, Darrell, 144
Trigano, 160–61
Triumph, 13, 18, 79, 135, 145, 148
Truman, Bill, 124
TT steeplechase, 138–39

U

Ubbiali, Carlo, 127
U.S. Grand Prix for Motocross, 131
U.S. Navy, 42, 44

V

Vehicle Identification Number, 107–108
velocipede, 1, 4–6
Vesco, Don, 125, 135
visibility, 52, 69
Voisin, Gabriel, 160

W

Wagar, Ivan, 34, 156, 163
Walker, Eugene, 134–35
Walker, Gene, 118
Walker, Otto, 113, 119
warranties, 25, 97
wartime use of motorcycles, 13, 18–19, 154
weather conditions, hazardous, 54, 66, 162
weight
    appropriate for rider, 24, 27
    effect of passenger, 76–77
    of Gyronaut, 159
    range available, 28–30, 32–33
Weishaar, Ray, 119
Wells, Gary, 152
wheelbase, 27, 38, 161
wheelies, 61–62, 153–54

wheels, 30–32, 40, 62, 77, 89, 162–63
    training, 8, 161, 163
    See also three-wheelers
Williams, Charles C., 147
Wolter, Joe, 122
Woods, Don, 140
Woodward, Doug, 144
Wright, J. S., 135

Yamaha Basic Rider Training Course,
    44, 49
Yamaha motorcycles, 79, 81, 135

Z

Zaum, Cecil, 51
Zels, Otto, 8–9
Z90 standard, 34